Pearson New International Edition

Action Research in Education
Ernie Stringer
Second Edition

Pearson Education Limited
Edinburgh Gate
Harlow
Essex CM20 2JE
England and Associated Companies throughout the world

Visit us on the World Wide Web at: www.pearsoned.co.uk

 ISBN 10: 1-292-04108-0
ISBN 13: 978-1-292-04108-7

British Library Cataloguing-in-Publication Data
A catalogue record for this book is available from the British Library

Printed in the United States of America

Table of Contents

The Purposes of Action Research

ACTION RESEARCH IN CLASSROOMS AND SCHOOLS

When teachers are asked to do action research in their classrooms, their response is likely to be a combination of surprise, disbelief, and/or wariness. Their responses are linked to images of research involving highly technical routines of investigation engaging sophisticated research instruments and complex statistical analysis. They cannot imagine that they would have the time or the inclination to engage in the highly technical research processes or to use the complex statistical analysis they imagine to be associated with research activities. They are also horrified at the prospect of adding more work to their already busy classroom routines, and can't imagine that "research" would serve any useful purpose in their teaching. The research studies they have read about in teacher preparation programs seem highly theoretical, and a considerable distance from the demanding realities of their daily classroom life.

Action research, however, is a distinctive approach to inquiry that is directly relevant to classroom instruction and learning and provides the means for teachers to enhance their teaching and improve student learning. Far from an "extra" that teachers must somehow cram into an already challenging work schedule, action research can be integrated into regular classroom activities to assist them to enhance student learning and improve their professional practice. The flexibility of action research, however, also provides others involved in schools—administrators, students, parents, school boards, and so on—with the means to solve many of the significant problems that are part of the complex life of a school.

In a recent research class I asked participants, all experienced teachers, to tell me why doing research was important for them. Some were concerned about the impact of current school practices on children and teachers, many of which they perceived as either damaging or inequitable. They wished to learn an approach to research that empowered teachers and children and enabled them to take control of their own teaching and learning, rather than being driven by the sometimes inappropriate dictates of a bureaucracy, or the lack of practical relevance of academic theory.

One class member, focusing on the administrative, organizational context of her work, talked of "the need to learn to think outside the hierarchy," making the familiar ways of organizing school life "strange." Her words echoed the sentiments of another class member who, speaking as a Hispanic person, realized how damaging research sometimes could be when information derived from generalized studies was applied inappropriately in particular classroom settings. She expressed that situation as "using research as a vehicle of oppression." Another, mindful of ways in which experts and administrators had impinged on his own professional life, expressed a concern that he might himself be guilty of the same crime. "How do I leave my own baggage behind in order to see the world [as it really is]?"

This was a common sentiment, expressed variously by individuals as the need to "change my mind-set," to be more alert, more sensitive, and to see more clearly what was happening to the children and colleagues with whom they worked. Others spoke of the need to be sensitive to their position as researchers, expressing a desire to "be a game-player with the people I'm working with," or "to sit with children and talk with them." All were concerned that their research work should have some practical outcome. As one indicated passionately, "I want to do research that will make a difference!" and another concurred, saying, "I want to have a positive effect for children." All saw action research, therefore, as a way of furthering their professional lines, enabling them to improve the educational experience of children in schools and having a beneficial impact on the lives of those with whom they worked.

Although there are limits on the time and resources available to engage research in everyday classroom and school life, by building their research capabilities teachers enhance their professional capabilities as they acquire and extend the skills and experience to engage in systematic investigation of significant issues. Action research is designed for practical purposes having direct and effective outcomes in the settings in which it is engaged. At the heart of the process, however, are teachers with the intent to investigate issues, which helps them to more effectively and efficiently engage the complex world of the classroom.

Action research is not just a formal process of inquiry, but may be applied systematically as a tool for learning in classrooms and schools. Sometimes referred to as inquiry learning, it is particularly relevant to those who engage in constructivist approaches to pedagogy. From an administrator's perspective, it is also a management tool, providing the means for developing effective plans, policies, programs, and procedures at classroom, school, or regional levels. Specific procedures, with relevant examples, of the ways action research processes assist educators to accomplish these types of activities. Although the application of systematic research processes sometimes requires a significant investment of time and resources, the pay-offs are considerable. Improved educational outcomes, highly engaged students, enthusiastic parents, and effective programs emerge that not only enhance the quality of student achievement, but also the quality of the educational life of all those who attend the school.

RESEARCH CONCEPTUALIZED

The Meriam-Webster Online Dictionary (2001) provides the following common ways of using the term "research":

1. the collecting of information about a particular subject
2. careful or diligent search

3. studious inquiry or examination
4. investigation or experimentation aimed at the discovery and interpretation of facts
5. revision of accepted theories or laws in the light of new facts
6. practical application of such new or revised theories or laws

Thus, when we research a particular topic for a school project, we are doing so in terms indicated by definition 1, collecting information in a general sense. Traditionally, research performed by scientists and scholars tended to be that related to definitions 4 and 5, though in recent times a broader use includes a more general sense of systematic inquiry inferred by definitions 2 and 3. When practitioners engage in *action* research, however, they add another dimension to the definition. They engage in careful, diligent inquiry, not for purposes of discovering new facts or revising accepted laws or theories, but to acquire information having practical application to the solution of specific problems related to their work. This text focuses on the latter use of the term, though its intent is to demonstrate how some of the tools of scientists and scholars may assist professionals to solve significant problems and to enhance their educational practices.

The deeper purpose of research is to extend people's knowledge and understanding, enabling them to make more informed choices and judgments about the complex issues embedded in their professional lives. Research increases the "stock of knowledge" that provides people with the means to expand their expertise and improve their professional capabilities. Understandings derived from research can provide people with new concepts, ideas, explanations, or interpretations that enable them to see the world in a different way and therefore approach situations in a new, hopefully better, way.

Though any type of learning may provide people with feelings of satisfaction, research provides the possibility of understandings that are truly transformational, requiring people to change the way they see the world. The physical sciences have many easily identified epiphanies, from Copernicus through Newton to Einstein and beyond, where scientific investigations transformed people's understanding of the nature of the physical universe. Though the human sciences have less definitive landmarks, the rigorous and systematic investigation of researchers has transformed the way people think about the social world. Rigorous studies by Kinsey, for instance, dramatically changed people's perception of human sexuality, and within education an emerging body of knowledge struggles to overcome the prejudices and preconceived notions of "common sense" often deeply embedded in the social consciousness of education. Research is a process of inquiry that refuses to accept the taken-for-granted, commonsense assumptions often enshrined in the fabric of any society, and holds them up for scrutiny, asking for observable and trustworthy evidence of "what is going on here."

Good research can be truly transformative, having the capacity to enable people to see the world in a different way—the effect of a truly "ah-haaa!" experience, when "the light bulb went on." It can thus be a epiphanic experience, and I have seen the excitement in people's eyes, heard the wonder in their voices, felt the sense of awe that sometimes comes with a new way of seeing, and occasionally, a new way of being. It encapsulates the old saying "the truth shall make you free!"

Research, more formally, may be defined as a process of systematic investigation leading to increased understanding of a phenomenon or issue of interest. Though research ultimately is quite an ordinary activity, a process for looking again at an existing situation (re-searching it) and seeing it in a different way, systematic processes of investigation provide the means for ensuring strong and effective processes of inquiry. Within the academic and professional worlds, however, two major systems of inquiry—paradigms—provide distinctly different ways in which to investigate phenomena in the physical and human universe. **Quantitative research,** or **scientific positivism** as it is more correctly known, and **naturalistic inquiry**—often referred to as **qualitative research**—provide powerful but different approaches to research. For purposes of clarity, the differences between the two paradigms, to provide researchers with clearer understandings about the nature of the investigations in which they are involved in their own classrooms and schools are also explored. As following sections indicate, action research has a history and tradition that differs significantly from other forms of research that have been commonly used to investigate educational issues.

AN ACTION RESEARCH ROUTINE: SYSTEMATIC PROCESSES OF INQUIRY

Although action research has much in common with the regular problem-solving and planning processes used by educators in the course of their daily classroom routine and school-work, its strength lies in its systematic execution of carefully articulated processes of inquiry. A simple "look-think-act" routine encapsulates the basic action research processes. As researchers implement a study they focus on a specific issue and then:

> **Look:** *Gathering information* (data) by careful observation that includes looking, listening, and recording.
> **Think:** *Analyzing* the information to identify significant features and elements.
> **Act:** Using that newly formulated information to *devise solutions* to the issue investigated.

This simple routine is enacted repeatedly, so that solutions are enacted, observed, analyzed, and reformulated until a successful outcome is achieved. An action research routine is therefore often depicted as a helix (Figure 1).

More complex problems and issues require more sophisticated formulations of this simple process, so that a fully articulated action research cycle incorporates the following processes:

- *Design the study*, carefully refining the issue to be investigated, planning systematic processes of inquiry, and checking the ethics and validity of the work.

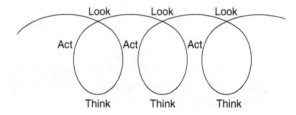

Figure 1
Action Research Helix

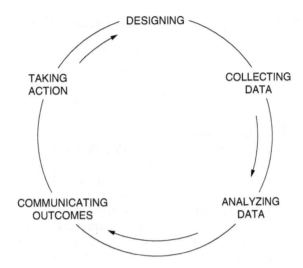

Figure 2
Action Research Cycle

- **Gather data,** including information from a variety of sources.
- **Analyze the data** to identify key features of the issue investigated.
- **Communicate** the outcomes of the study to relevant audiences.
- **Use** the outcomes of the study to work toward resolution of the issue investigated.

The cyclical nature of these processes may usefully be depicted as shown in Figure 2. For clarity of detail, however, steps in the action research cycle may also be presented as a sequence, as in Figure 3. As the figure illustrates, action research is distinguished from basic research by an "action" phase of inquiry. Although basic research provides information not necessarily used in the research context, action research always has an immediate practical or applied purpose.

USING ACTION RESEARCH

Action research has a wide range of applications in classroom, school, and community contexts. Action research provides the basis for formulating effective solutions to highly significant classroom and school problems—such as classes that are particularly fractious, exceptionally problematic groups of students, underachieving students, multiple external demands, and so on. Action research also provides a useful tool for day-to-day planning in classrooms, such as in lesson planning, formulation of teaching strategies, and student assessment, or more extensive tasks such as syllabus planning, curriculum construction, and evaluation. For the school administrator, action research is also a management tool, providing the means to systematically resolve difficult situations, to engage in program development and evaluation, or to develop strategic initiatives with families and the community.

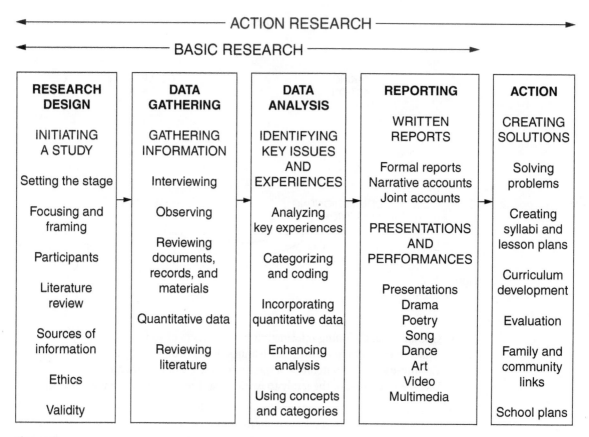

Figure 3
Action Research Sequence

A small sample of action research projects in schools, universities, and community contexts includes the following:

- A young teacher, concerned by the disciplinary problems she experienced with a group of "at-risk" boys in her classroom, engaged in an action research process that revealed to her a very different understanding of these children. The knowledge she gained changed her view of the problems she was experiencing, leading to dramatic changes in the way she approached her teaching.
- A grade 3 teacher, concerned that the district was cutting funds for art in schools, investigated with her students the part art played in their classroom lives. They produced an illustrated booklet and a mural for presentation to the district superintendent.
- A teacher engaged in action research processes with his students to construct and implement class syllabi, achieving high levels of student engagement and exciting learning outcomes.
- A neighborhood group engaged in participatory action research with principals, teachers, and parents to investigate ways of increasing parental involvement in local schools. Between them they produced a highly useful list of actions to be taken by teachers and parents.

- A school hired a consultant to assist faculty in evaluating the school's programs. Using action research, the consultant worked with teachers, administrators, and students to highlight positive features of the school's operation and to reveal issues and challenges needing to be addressed.
- A university department used action research processes to plan the implementation of a large, new program to integrate technology into educational areas. The project was highly successful in terms of the levels of engagement of participants and the outcomes achieved.
- A school used action research to resolve racial problems that threatened the stability of school life. A teacher assisted a group of students to investigate related issues in their school and community, leading to a new program aimed at ameliorating problems the school had experienced.
- Two middle school teachers used action research processes to investigate issues of harassment and prejudice with middle school students. Following processes of exploration, students in both groups identified key features of these issues and used them as the basis for producing and staging highly informative plays.

Case Study: Teacher Action Research

The following story and the examples provide some indication of the potential rewards to be attained as educators become sophisticated researchers in their own right. The stories illustrate how classroom teachers have added to their repertoire of professional skills, and in the process made their work more productive, successful, and enjoyable.

Student Apathy: A Teacher Studies Her Classroom

By Lorise Dorry

A month into a new school year I was puzzled by my inability to engage the students in my year 6 elementary class in a poorer suburb of a large city. In my fifth year of teaching, I felt myself to be a competent and experienced teacher, now well able to handle the rigorous daily routines of working with a large group of children. Despite careful creative planning, however, the students seemed to lack the life and vitality I had experienced in other classes. While they were not badly behaved children, they seemed to be merely "going through the motions," were apt to be a little cynical about the work I prescribed, and "smart" comments intruded into their classroom discussions with some degree of regularity. Despite instituting a number of classroom management techniques and attempting to find interesting ways to present the work, I found them decidedly apathetic. Nothing I tried, it seemed, had any impact on the dull listlessness with which they greeted each new learning activity, or enticed them to improve the rather mediocre work they consistently produced.

Six weeks into the semester, experiencing some degree of frustration and increasing levels of anxiety about my capabilities as a teacher, I decided the time had come to investigate the situation more thoroughly. Using an action research routine I had learned at college, I systematically planned how I would seek to gain greater understanding about how and why it was that my students were so apathetic in class. I began to observe my class more carefully, noting the ways different students went about their work; when, where, and how they engaged in the different classroom activities; their responses to different events occurring within the classroom; and the ways in which different individuals and groups interacted. In doing so I gained greater insights into the social dynamics of my classroom, noting those students who tended to "hang" together, individuals who seemed to be the natural leaders, and those who were isolates—the informal social groups and leaders that are part of any social situation. Over the following weeks I also found opportunities to meet informally with a number of students—leaders and members from the different informal groups—chatting with them in the schoolyard, corridors, and in "downtimes" in the classroom. I gradually accumulated information that enabled me to understand my classroom from the children's perspective and gained much deeper insights into what was affecting my children's classroom life.

Wishing to take advantage of the new insights into my students' experience, I decided to engage the class in a research project as part of the literacy objectives of my class syllabus. I explained to them my concerns about their apparent lack of interest in their schoolwork and my desire to have them assist me in exploring the issue. Using small focus groups, I provided time for students to talk about this issue and list the major features of their experience. As the list of issues emerged I noticed how negative the comments seemed:

- *The work we do in class is boring.*
- *We don't like the reading we have to do each day.*
- *Math is too difficult.*
- *Its embarrassing when Mrs. Dorry comments on our work.*
- *We have the comments some students make about us.*

And so on.

A little perturbed by the negative tone of their comments, I asked students to return to their groups to discuss whether there was anything they liked about the class. Feedback sessions revealed a number of aspects of their class experience they enjoyed:

- *The computer lab is cool.*
- *The last social studies project was awesome.*
- *We like it when we can work in groups.*
- *We really like Mrs. Dorry.*

And so on.

The following day I returned to the issues with the whole class, asking them to talk about those they considered most important. Gradually a consensus emerged that "boring class work" was a major issue. Further group discussions identified the areas of work and the type of activities they found boring. In the process, some children started to spontaneously suggest ways they could make their work more interesting. At that stage I suggested that students form work groups to investigate ways they could make work in those areas more interesting. Different groups focused on reading and literature, social studies, math, and science worked excitedly as they came up with "bright ideas" drawn from their previous classroom experiences, from ideas they'd heard other students or family talk of, or from their own creative imagination.

Sessions in following days provided opportunities for each group to present their ideas to the whole class, and for other students to provide suggestions for extending or enhancing the learning content or activities being presented. The process was not straightforward for all groups. The math group, for instance, required considerable attention, and I discovered I needed to provide a simple explanation of the purposes and content of the math syllabus to the work group. I discovered, however, that this provided them with a much deeper understanding of math as an area of study, an understanding that was passed on to the rest of the class in feedback sessions.

In the following weeks, I was able to work with the class, providing simple descriptions of the syllabus for each of the content areas and having the students assist me to show how they could attain the objectives through learning activities they were largely able to define themselves. As they engaged the process, I noticed increasing levels of engagement, as students not only became absorbed in the learning activities they had helped devise, but also became excited about their achievements. They also, in the process, dealt with some of the behavioral problems that had been noted in their initial discussions, devising a "code of conduct" that, amongst other things, prohibited "putting down" remarks or comments likely to embarrass individuals.

Within a few weeks of starting the process, I was able to reflect on what the class had accomplished under my guidance. Most of the students were engaged in their work most of the time, they appeared happy with and interested in the work they were doing, and the quality of their work had risen dramatically. Eventually I started getting positive comments from parents indicating they were aware of the differences in their children's responses to school. "I don't know what you've done," said one parent with a laugh, "But I have to stop Clyde from coming to school at daybreak!" My principal and fellow teachers also noted the difference. One commented, "That class has been difficult to work with for years. You've certainly made a difference. What are you doing?"

By the end of the year, comparing results on tests from previous years, I was able to take satisfaction in noting the gains accomplished in many areas by many of the students, and the excitement and enthusiasm that permeated my class for much of the day. By having the class assist me to systematically investigate the problem I had identified, I was not only able to understand more clearly the nature of the problem, but to engage my students in helping plan solutions to the problems that emerged during our research.

CHARACTERISTICS OF ACTION RESEARCH

Action research has a long history, one often associated with the work of Kurt Lewin, who viewed action research as a cyclical, dynamic, and collaborative process in which people addressed social issues affecting their lives. Through cycles of planning, acting, observing, and reflecting, participants sought changes in practices leading to social action for improvement. A form of action research was used to address problems of assimilation, segregation, and discrimination, assisting people to resolve issues, initiate change, and study the impact of those changes (Lewin, 1938, 1946, 1948; Lewin & Lewin, 1942). His approach to action research is reflected in the definition given by Bogdan and Biklen (1992), "the systematic collection of information that is designed to bring about social change."

THE PURPOSES OF ACTION RESEARCH

Noffke (1997), however, suggests that action research is best thought of as a large family, one in which beliefs and relationships vary greatly (p. 306).

Kemmis and McTaggart (1988) suggest that action research is a "form of collective, self-reflective enquiry undertaken by participants in social situations in order to improve the rationality and justice of their own social or educational practices, as well as their understanding of these practices and the situations in which these practices are carried out" (p. 6). For Kemmis and McTaggart, research is carried out by any group with a shared concern, and is only action research when it is collaborative.

Reason and Bradbury (2001, p.10) extend this vision by describing action research as "a participatory, democratic process concerned with developing practical knowing in the pursuit of worthwhile human purposes, grounded in a participatory worldview which we believe is emerging at this historical moment. It seeks to bring together action and reflection, theory and practice, in participation with others, in the pursuit of practical solutions to issues of pressing concern to people, and more generally the flourishing of individual persons and their communities." For them, action research requires skills and methods to enable researchers to foster an inquiring approach to their own practices, to engage in face-to-face work with others to address issues of mutual concern, and to create a wider community of inquiry involving whole organizations.

The relevance of action research to education is signaled in the recent proliferation of texts in this area. They cover a diverse range of orientations and methodologies that reflect the different purposes and theoretical orientations of the authors, and lead to quite different sets of practices. Much action research in education is teacher-centered, focusing on teacher reflection, instructional practices, and evaluation of student outcomes. More sophisticated forms of action research engage collaborative practices that may include any combination of students, colleagues, administrators, parents, and the community.

Texts that focus on the use of action research to improve teacher practices and/or student outcomes include those by Johnson (2002); Johnson (2007); Koshy (2005); Mertler (2005); Calhoun (1994); Brown and Dowling (1998); and Burnaford, Fischer, and Hobson (2000). Literature that provides a broader orientation to the use of action research in school settings—such as applications to broader curriculum and ethical and legal issues—includes Holly, Arhar, and Kasten (2004); Armstrong (2004); Bray, Lee, Smith, and Yorks (2000); Tomai (2003); Mills (2007); Anderson, Herr, and Nihlen (2007); and Somekh (2005). In the same vein, Meyers and Rust (2003) and McNiff and Whitehead (2006) describe how teachers can use action research to tackle basic classroom issues, design their own professional development, and reshape instructional practices. Kalmbach, Phillips, and Carr (2006) describe how action research can serve as a vehicle for assuming a professional identity for students seeking initial teaching licensure. McClean, Herman, and Herman (2005) reveal the way teachers and administrators adopt action research as a strategy for taking a more active role in determining the best solutions to problems in schools.

Literature that focuses more broadly on school improvement or change and development includes Sagor (2000), who provides a seven-step process for improving teaching and learning, and Glanz (2003), who focuses on improvements to the work community within a school. Some of the literature is more clearly directed to educational change, sometimes incorporating social change as an essential element of an action research process (Atweh, Kemmis, & Weeks, 2005; Berge & Ve, 2000; Brown & Jones, 2002; Christiansen,

Goulet, Krentz, & Maeers, 1997; Fals-Borda & Rahman, 1991; O'Hanlon, 2003). Pedraza and Rivera (2005) likewise focus on school reform through educational research with and for Latino communities.

Other texts focus on specific areas of educational life. Burns (1999) presents action research as a collaborative process emerging from the common concerns of English language teachers; Wallace (1998) shows how language teachers can develop their expertise; and Sykes (2002) shows how media specialists can convince their constituents of the importance of school libraries as technology drastically transforms the way information is stored, accessed, and used.

International perspectives are presented by Hollingsworth (1997), who demonstrates how practioners are influencing policy by conducting research, and McTaggart (1997), who describes the development of democratic research practice in quite different institutional and cultural contexts.

Though many authors incorporate quantitative data into an action research process, most recognize it as a naturalistic approach to research that engages teachers in reflective processes that illuminate significant features of their classroom practice. The approach to action research presented in this text differs from much of the literature on teacher research or practitioner research in that it does not focus solely on the teacher, though teachers are central participants in the process. The orientation to action research described herein focuses on:

1. **Change:** Improving practices and behaviors by changing them.
2. **Reflection:** People thinking, reflecting, and/or theorizing about their own practices, behaviors, and situations.
3. **Participation:** People changing their own practices and behaviors, not those of others.
4. **Inclusion:** Starting with the agendas and perspectives of the least powerful, widening the circle to include all those affected by the problem.
5. **Sharing:** People sharing their perspectives with others.
6. **Understanding:** Achieving clarity of understanding of the different perspectives and experiences of all involved.
7. **Repetition:** Repeating cycles of research activity leading toward the solution to a problem.
8. **Practice:** Testing emerging understandings by using them as the basis for changing practices or constructing new practices.
9. **Community:** Working toward the development/construction of a learning community.

WORKING DEVELOPMENTALLY: ENLARGING THE CIRCLE OF INQUIRY

Although action research works effectively for discrete problems and issues within classrooms, it has the potential for more extended applications across classrooms, within schools, or within a community. As participants cycle through a research process, increasing understandings reveal related issues going beyond the immediate focus of investigation, pointing to productive possibilities that might emerge by increasing the scope and power of inquiry. Investigation of specific problems often reveals the multiple dimensions of the situation requiring attention, and investigation of each of those dimensions further illuminates the situation, revealing further possibilities for action.

The process of "starting small" and increasing the breadth and complexity of activity, I call "working developmentally." This is very different from developmental psychology or child development, which is an integral part of most education programs, though conceptually there are some similarities. In each, it is important to engage learners at the level they are capable of comprehending and achieving, according to their stage of "development." In participatory action research, a study may start with limited objectives but the scope of the study may be extended as understanding and awareness increase. The potential for positive change and development increases exponentially as increasing numbers of people and issues are included.

When Shelia Baldwin's group (Baldwin, 1997) investigated the problem of racial disharmony in their school, for instance, they discovered the need to increase the scope of their investigation to include their homes and neighborhoods. The understandings emerging from these investigations greatly increased the power of their investigation and provided the basis for schoolwide action.

In similar fashion, girls involved in the sexual harassment study first increased the number of girls involved, then discovered the need to include boys as part of the group. Investigation of group members' own experiences eventually revealed the need to communicate with other people, including school administrators and security officers. Eventually, they were able to take actions that enabled them to inform all people within the school of the outcomes of their investigation, and to see quite dramatic changes emerge from their efforts.

A key feature of the developmental process is to start with limited objectives. Although many problems within schools, such as high drop-out rates or low student achievement, are complex and multidimensional in scope, it is best to focus initial inquiries on some tangible and achievable objectives. Small initial gains provide people with the stimulus of success and inspire them to take further action. By engaging in continuous cycles of the "look-think-act" process they are able to encompass more dimensions of the problem and increased levels of engagement. Eventually they may be able to incorporate other stakeholders—teachers, administrators, family, and community—thus marshalling increased levels of support and resources that extend the power of the actions they take (See Figure 4).

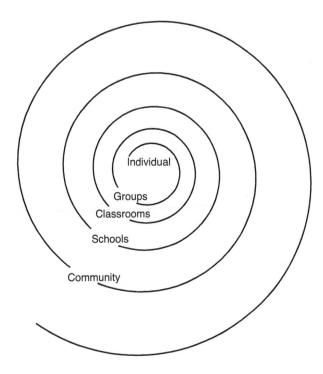

Figure 4
Action Research Spiral

SUMMARY

The Purposes of Action Research

Action research is a process of systematic inquiry.

The purpose of action research is to provide educational practitioners with new knowledge and understanding, enabling them to improve educational practices or resolve significant problems in classrooms and schools.

Action research derives from a research tradition emphasizing cyclical, dynamic, and collaborative approaches to investigation.

A common process of inquiry includes:

- Design of the study
- Data gathering
- Data analysis
- Communicating outcomes
- Taking action

Action research may be engaged as a developmental process that systematically increases the scope of the investigation.

Understanding Action Research: Paradigms and Methods

Understanding Action Research: Paradigms and Methods

INTRODUCTION: TEACHING AS A PROCESS OF INQUIRY

The public perception of teaching is that it is a simple task, merely requiring the teacher to present information to students, have them learn it, and test them to see that they have learned it. As teachers know, teaching and learning is a much more complex task requiring an extended body of professional knowledge that can be applied to the formulation of effective learning processes for students. Teachers are confronted by a diversity of students who differ markedly in what they bring to the classroom in terms of their ability levels, gender, personalities, family environment, socioeconomic status, and ethnic and cultural backgrounds.

There is no "one-size-fits-all" formula that teachers can apply to their teaching in all situations. Thus, the first task of a teacher—one that becomes an ongoing part of classroom life—is to engage in systematic processes of inquiry and planning. Some of the basic questions that teachers must ask are:

- Who are these children?
- How old are they?
- What are the attributes of the children I will need to take into account in planning a program of learning for them? Age? Ability levels? Gender? Ethnicity? Family background? Health? And so on.

The nature of the curriculum itself also will be subject to conscious processes of inquiry. Teachers will plan a program of learning and devise strategies of teaching and learning according to the content areas to be taught, specified state standards, the age/grade level of the class, and the appropriate strategies of teaching and accompanying learning activities. Their initial inquiries into teaching a class will be based on questions such as the following:

- What is to be taught (to these children, at this level)?
- How can it be taught?

- Which teaching strategies will be appropriate?
- Which learning activities will be effective?

Teachers therefore must engage in systematic processes of inquiry as an ongoing feature of their classroom life in order to enable their students to attain effective learning outcomes. Action research therefore provides them with a framework of activities that enables them to systematically accomplish these tasks. It provides the means for them, over a period of time, to build a body of knowledge about the students in their care, and to incorporate it into an effective program of teaching and learning.

The need for action research applies not only to classroom teachers, but also to administrators who, like teachers, confront complex problems in planning the ongoing organization and operation of a school. They must deal with the diverse attributes of the children in the school, the teachers that comprise their staff, the parents of the children, and the particular communities in which their school is located. Systematic processes of inquiry will, over time, provide them with a wealth of information that contributes to the operation of a harmonious and highly productive educational environment.

Action research as an approach to inquiry provides information that is very specific to the particular situations that confront teachers or administrators, and provides the means to devise actions that are effective in that context. This context-relevant information stands alongside of the more generalized body of knowledge within the research literature that is incorporated into their professional preparation and development.

Because of the diversity of approaches to research now associated with education, this chapter will clarify the distinction between the major paradigms—research systems—that now comprise the literature. The action research enacted by teachers and principals, although having some of the major attributes of a good research process, differs in purpose and outcomes from that embodied in the research literature. While the former is designed to produce practical outcomes relevant to a specific classroom or school, the research literature provides a more general body of knowledge that can be applied across a wide spectrum of locations and contexts. As becomes clear when we learn more about action research, one of its functions is to provide teachers and principals with the means to test the relevance of the research literature to the particular contexts in which they work.

The body of professional knowledge contained within the research literature largely is the product of two different *paradigms* that signal distinctively different approaches to investigation. One, often called *quantitative research,* but more properly known as objective science or scientific positivism, is a hallmark of the modern world. The other paradigm, often called *qualitative research,* though more correctly labeled naturalistic inquiry, is a more recent addition to the research arena. Action research, although it often makes use of quantitative or statistical information, is more clearly associated with the latter paradigm. As we engage in any form of research we need to keep clear the different intentions of our research to ensure that we enact appropriate procedures that enable us to attain the purposes we seek to accomplish.

OBJECTIVE SCIENCE AND EXPERIMENTAL RESEARCH

A large body of educational research based on the application of the procedures of objective science provides an enduring and powerful base of professional knowledge for teachers, administrators, and others with interests in education. It results from one of the enduring legacies of the modern world that is bestowed by science—the application of the scientific method to the solution of problems. So successful has science been at providing miraculous material benefits to human life that billions of dollars are now routinely invested in scientific research, and education has benefited greatly from this systematic investigation of problems and issues related to teaching and learning.

This body of "scientific" knowledge derives from a philosophical perspective that is technically known as scientific positivism. Scientific positivism operates according to a particular set of underlying assumptions and beliefs about the way knowledge can be acquired. It assumes a fixed universe—that events occur in stable and predictable ways according fundamental laws that govern the operation of all things. Scientific positivism assumes that ultimately, in principle, everything in the universe can be measured with precision, and the relationship between things can be described accurately. Continuing scientific efforts to refine and extend our understanding of the universe are carried out in the disciplinary spheres of physics, chemistry, biology, and so on. Each has a distinctive focus, providing scientifically verified information that extends our understanding of the physical universe. Physiology and human biology focus on those aspects of the universe dealing with the human body, but generally stop short of involvement of the "mind," that aspect of the universe that is peculiar to human beings.

The purpose of scientific inquiry, therefore, is to describe with precision the features of the universe in which we live, and the stable relationships that hold between those features. Scientific work is therefore often associated with accurate definition and measurement of "variables"—the features that comprise the universe. The ultimate goal of such work is to establish causal connections that enable us to say that "If x occurs, then y will follow (in all places, at all times)"—for example, if you heat a metal it will expand at a particular rate; if you cool water to a certain temperature it will turn into a solid. Our ability to describe the universe in these terms is responsible for the miraculous transformation of the material environment—aircraft, computers, motor vehicles, fabrics, construction materials, household goods—as well as huge improvements in health and longevity. Many diseases that once ravaged whole regions of the world have now been eradicated, and medications provide the means to alleviate a host of ailments to which humans are susceptible. All result from the careful application of the scientific method to the description of the laws governing the physical universe.

The outcome of the application of scientific principles to the development of explanation and understanding is a highly sophisticated and rigorous stock of scientific knowledge resulting in many advances in policies, practices, and technologies across all areas of human life. The knowledge emerging from positivistic science continues to have the potential to dramatically enhance people's lives.

The primary method for establishing scientific explanations is the experimental method. Experiments are carefully designed so that random assignment of subjects to experimental groups and the controlled application of experimental treatments or interventions allows researchers to state with high degrees of certainty that the effects observed were related to the treatments or interventions. Many studies, for instance, have observed the effect of different teaching strategies on student learning, with researchers carefully controlling the conditions under which these strategies were applied in classrooms to carefully selected groups of students, and the experiments operating in carefully controlled classroom conditions. The intent of such designs is to attempt to eliminate rival explanations for the results obtained. Controlling extraneous variables is thus an important aspect of experimental design, since the potential influences on learning are many and varied, including such variables as class size, student learning styles, ethnicity, race, gender, social class, type of school, parenting style experienced by students, motivation, personality, illness, drug use, intelligence, aptitude, school size, exposure to media, and so on. Researchers want to be sure that any result they obtain from experimentally manipulating teaching strategies may not, in fact, be attributable to one or more of these or any other factors. The body of knowledge derived from these studies enables educational practitioners to analyze problems occurring in a classroom, to identify the factors likely to be their cause, and to formulate actions that will provide a remedy.

Quasi-experiments, or nonexperiments as they are sometimes called (Johnson, 2001), are used where it is not possible to manipulate variables experimentally, either for ethical or pragmatic reasons. It would be difficult, for instance, to imagine setting up a study in which students were subject to intense pain to see whether that factor increased their performance on tests. What is possible, in these situations, is to engage in studies where variables are controlled or manipulated statistically rather than experimentally, establishing the nature of the relationship between variables by carefully contrived statistical manipulation. Researchers are able to employ statistical methods that control for a wide range of variables and, in the process, minimize the plausibility of rival explanations for the effects observed.

McEwan (2000) provides a clear description of quasi-experimental studies of school voucher programs, showing how in conditions where it is not possible to control who enters private and public schools, researchers are able to employ statistical methods that control for the background of families and students. In this manner it is possible to minimize the possibility of plausible rival explanations for the effects of school voucher programs and to control for the effect of variables such as parental education, family income, gender, race, and ethnicity.

Both experimental and quasi-experimental research are subject to forms of quality control to ensure rigor in procedure and stability of results. For these reasons, experiments are evaluated according to their reliability, internal validity, and external validity—the extent to which similar results may be obtained from different settings, samples, and times (reliability); the extent to which results might be attributed to the experimental variables (internal validity); and the extent to which results apply to the broader population from which the sample was drawn (external validity or generalizability).

Experimental and quasi-experimental research have provided a large array of information having the potential to dramatically improve people's social health and well-being. As will become evident in the following discussion, however, health problems continue to proliferate, despite the huge array of scientifically validated knowledge now at our disposal. Although scientific positivism has provided a powerful body of knowledge about the operation of the nature of the physical environment and the human body, the operation of the physical environment and the human body, it is clear that this approach to research is limited in its ability to explain human conduct, as will become evident in the sections that follow.

The application of scientific principles through experimental and quasi-experimental studies has obvious implications for education. If we can scientifically measure and describe the precise nature of the learning process, then we should, in theory, be able to control all of the factors likely to influence a student's learning and therefore produce a highly effective education for each and every person. Armed with scientific knowledge, we should be able to predict with precision the conditions required for any child to acquire the knowledge necessary to achieve success in education, irrespective of his or her gender, class, ethnicity, or any other factor likely to impinge on learning. As the following section reveals, however, understanding human social and cultural behavior has proven much more elusive, and other research strategies have emerged to provide different but effective ways of understanding educational issues and problems.

UNDERSTANDING HUMAN SOCIAL LIFE: NATURALISTIC INQUIRY

The problem with applying science to human affairs lies in the nature of humanity. We are at once physical, biological, and sociocultural beings, and attempts to understand our behavior need to take into account each of those facets. While the methods of positivistic science are powerful ways of understanding our physical being, and provide deep insights into our biologic nature, they come up short as vehicles for providing explanations for the sociocultural aspects of human life. Although experimentation still assists us to understand certain features of human social and cultural life, positivistic explanations, ultimately, must fail to encompass some of the fundamental features of human life—the creative construction of meaning that is at the center of every social activity. It is the need to investigate meaning that is at the heart of naturalistic inquiry—in classroom terms, the different ways that teachers and students experience classroom events, and the meaning they attach to them.

While experimental science, therefore, has provided much useful information, the reality of this knowledge, however, is that any theory of human behavior can only be a tentative, partial explanation of any individual's or group's actions or behaviors. Two things intervene in attempts to describe scientific laws of human behavior. One is the nature of human beings themselves. As cross-cultural studies have demonstrated convincingly, people perceive the world and respond to it in many different ways. Given the same sets of "facts," people will interpret both what they are seeing and what that means in many different ways. No amount of explanation or clarification can provide an ultimate truth about the way people should behave, since behavior is predicated on sets of beliefs that are not, in principle, verifiable. Any "truth" of human experience is true only within a given framework of meanings.

This becomes increasingly clear if we consider some of the fundamental conditions of human social life and the way they impact the lives of individuals. The concept of the life-world comes to us from the work of sociologists such as Peter Berger (Berger, Berger, & Kellner, 1973; Berger & Luckmann, 1967) who engage research from the perspective that people construct reality as an ongoing social process in their everyday lives. The life-world refers to the consciousness of everyday life carried by every individual that provides coherence and order to our existence. The life-world is not a genetically inherited view of the world, but is learned by individuals as they experience everyday events and interactions within the environments of their families and communities. The life-world is therefore socially constructed, so that individuals learn to live in a social world according to sets of meaning, deeply embedded in their everyday conduct, that are shared by others living in that particular place and time.

The life-world is not a random set of events, but is given order and coherence by a patterned, structured organization of meaning that is so "ordinary" that people literally do not see, or usually do not consciously realize, the depth and complexity of the worlds they inhabit. A child learns to associate with parents and siblings in particular ways, to communicate using a particular language, to act in particular ways, and to participate in events such as meals, conversation, play, work, and so on using appropriate behaviors and routine ways of accomplishing his or her tasks of everyday life. Like a fish in the sea, people cannot see the "water" of this patterned, structured everyday life, but live in a taken-for-granted social world providing order and coherence for every aspect of their everyday lives—the interactions, acts, activities, events, purposes, feelings, and productions that comprise their lives.

We get some idea of what this means when we visit a new place for the first time, especially if it is in a foreign country. We feel uncomfortable to varying degrees until we learn the "rules" that enable us to operate in the new setting—the appropriate words to use, how sit or stand, how to eat, how to dress appropriately, and so on. We become aware of a myriad of small behaviors that those living in the context take for granted because it is so much an ordinary part of their life-world.

I remember people's consternation when I visited an Aboriginal community for the first time and sat with my wife in church, not realizing that the sexes had been strictly segregated and that I was sitting with the women. I've also entered a school staffroom and felt the embarrassed silence when I inadvertently sat in "Mr Jeffries's chair." Small and apparently inconsequential behaviors can sometimes have quite a dramatic impact on our ability to interact comfortably with people.

Anthropologist Goodenough (1971) conceptualized this life-world in terms of the concept of culture, which he defines as the socially learned rules and boundaries that enable a person to know what *is* (how the world is *defined*, structured, made up), what *can be* (what is *possible* in the world, whether it be ancestral ghosts, the existence of God, or faster-than-light travel), what *should be* (the system of values enabling the individual to distinguish between good and bad, appropriate and inappropriate), *what to do* (what acts or behaviors are required to accomplish a purpose), and *how to do it* (the steps required to accomplish that purpose). Individuals, therefore, inhabit a life-world comprised of taken-for-granted rules and boundaries giving order and coherence to their lives. Without these patterns and structures of meaning, people would live in a bewildering, chaotic world of sensation and events that would make human life as we know it impossible. It is this cultural cradle that enables us to live together in harmony, to accomplish day-to-day tasks such as eating meals, dressing, communicating through talk and discussion, working, resolving disputes, and mowing the lawn.

The distinctive aspect of our cultural life-world is that we share it with people who have learned similar sets of meanings and who act according to the patterns and structures of meaning with those who have had similar life experiences. But beneath the apparent order and coherence of the social life-world is a deeply chaotic system of meanings that continually threatens the possibility of an ordered and productive daily life. For each person has had somewhat different experiences, and each has built a system of meanings that works superficially to accomplish ordinary tasks, but has slightly different nuances and interpretations that at any one time can be magnified and distorted, causing confusion or conflict as people try to accomplish their everyday lives.

This is readily apparent when people get married and discover that a person with whom they thought they shared deeply consonant views of the world evinces actions and behaviors not in accord with their own. Small acts, the dropping of a sock or tissue, the use of a word, can trigger discomfort, discordance, and even conflict. The art of marriage requires people to learn new sets of meaning, to negotiate actions and behaviors consonant with a partner's existing habits and values, in order to accomplish a life together. It is something that is sometimes astonishingly difficult, even for people closely committed to each other.

Teachers, likewise, interact with students who often come from significantly different social and cultural backgrounds, and who define and respond to events in the classroom according to a wide range of expectations, beliefs, and perceptions. Finding a way of building a repetoire of classroom activities and rules to govern a well-ordered classroom requires a sensitive understanding of these diverse sets of meanings. One of a teacher's major tasks is to uncover the meanings implicit in the acts and behaviors of students, and through that increased understanding to seek ways of enacting classroom activities that will "make sense" to them.

This is not just a technical task, but involves deeply held feelings associated with the meanings implicit in a person's life-world. Not only are people attached to their particular life-worlds emotionally, they also react unfavorably when their life-world is threatened. A denial of the veracity or validity of any aspect of a person's life-world is likely to create negative feelings that inhibit the possibility of productivity. The world of human life is meaningful, interactional, emotional, and constructive, and accomplishing productive and harmonious human activity requires all these aspects of experience to be taken into account. It is this understanding that is at the heart of action research—the need to clarify and understand the meaning implicit in the actions and behaviors of all people involved in events on which research is focused, and to use those extended understandings as the basis for devising effective and productive classroom and school routines and activities.

This lesson is deeply inscribed in my consciousness. As a young teacher I worked with the children of Australian Aboriginal people who lived a very traditional hunter-gatherer lifestyle. It soon became evident to me that they literally lived in a different universe—that the way they viewed the world, the way they acted toward each other, and their aspirations and responses were so dramatically different from my own that my teaching made absolutely no "sense" to their everyday world. I became aware of the need to come to know something of that world in order to provide a bridge of understanding between their world and the curriculum that I was teaching.

Even the simplest aspects of the syllabus entailed elements that were deeply engaged with the different visions of the world and the lifestyles attached. As I watched the people engaged in the simple act of gathering seeds and fruit from the plants in the desert to provide for their immediate needs, I became aware of how deeply embedded I was in the world of technological production when I cut a slice of bread for my lunch. Behind that simple act lay the mining and production of metals needed for the knife, as well as that required for the production of the machinery needed to grow and process the wheat, and to fabricate the ovens and other machinery needed to make the bread. What I had seen as a simple loaf of bread became a complex technological production.

My eyes began to see a different world when I asked the question, "What do I need to know in order to understand where this bread came from?" A very different order of understanding came to mind when I asked, "What do Aboriginal people need to know when they ask a similar question about their own foodstuffs?" Not only does the actual world of technological production intrude, but the web of work and economic relationships enabling me to acquire that loaf of bread is likewise complex, and very different from the web of relationships surrounding Aboriginal meals.

This experience changed forever the way I see teaching. I now realize the need to find ways of making connections between what my students know—how they perceive and understand the world from the standpoint of their own history of experience—what they need to learn, and how they can learn it. That fundamental perception has been recently reinforced as I've worked in schools in the United States, where the experiences and perspectives of Hispanic and African American students and community people has enriched and challenged my educational endeavors. As I worked in the South Valley in Albuquerque and the poorer suburbs of Columbia and Richmond, I had learning work to do before I could frame my knowledge in ways that made sense to people in those places. As a teacher I had to do some on-the-spot research to enable me to do my work effectively.

Differences in cultural perspective do not relate to ethnic differences alone, however. We have only to look at the differences in the way teenagers and their parents interpret events to realize the extent to which their age differences create differences in cultural experience and perspective in everyday life. Parents listening to their children's music often shake their heads in wonder that *anyone* could find the experience pleasurable—a response shared by teenagers listening to their parent's music. They all are hearing the same music, in terms of the sounds emanating from the instrument or recording, but they have very different experiences of the sounds, and associate very different meanings with them.

OBJECTIVE SCIENCE AND NATURALISTIC INQUIRY: A COMPARISON

Objective science and **naturalistic inquiry** provide quite different approaches to research. Both provide the means for teachers and other educational practitioners to acquire knowledge and understanding that assists them to accomplish their complex professional duties. As the previous discussion has indicated, however, they have quite different purposes, processes, and outcomes, the first being to acquire objective, factual information about a limited number of variables, and the second to understand more clearly the multiple dimensions of socially constructed human behavior. Theses attributes are summarized in Figure 1.

We need to be wary of setting up boundaries that make too fixed the distinctions between the two paradigms. Qualitative research does, for instance, sometimes make use of statistical data to extend or clarify information emerging in the research process. Conversely, quantitative researchers sometimes engage in preliminary qualitative studies to identify the variables to be included in their research. Neither paradigm is right or wrong, better or worse. Each seeks to attain different purposes, using different processes to attain

OBJECTIVE SCIENCE	NATURALISTIC INQUIRY
Purposes	**Purposes**
Studies events and behaviors *objectively*.	Studies people's *subjective* experience.
Hypothesizes a relationship between variables of interest.	*Explores perspectives* on an issue or problem.
Processes	**Processes**
Precisely *measures* quantities of variables.	*Describes* people's experience and perspective of the issue/problem.
Carefully *controls* events and conditions within the study.	Allows events to unfold *naturally*.
Uses *statistical analysis* of data.	Uses *interpretive methods* to analyze the data.
Outcomes	**Outcomes**
Seeks *explanations* for events and behaviors.	Seeks to *understand* events and behaviors.
Describes *causes* of events and behaviors.	Constructs *detailed descriptions* of events and behaviors.
Generalizes findings to sites and people not included in the study.	Findings are *setting and person specific*.

Figure 1
Objective Science and Naturalistic Inquiry

different types of outcome.[1] Each is evaluated by different sets of criteria to determine the strength, quality, or rigor of the research.

To ensure that their research does not become caught in the muddy waters between the paradigms, however, researchers need to frequently ask themselves "What is the purpose or

---

[1]Distinguishing between different research paradigms is not always straightforward. The problem partially relates to the rather loose use of associated terminology, where the literature often refers to *quantitative* and *qualitative* methods as equivalent to the distinction between objective science and naturalistic inquiry and fails to differentiate between the research *paradigm* and the research *methods*. There is a difference, for instance, between qualitative *research* and qualitative *methods*. It is possible to use qualitative methods to acquire and partially analyze data in experimental science—to use qualitative data objectively. Conversely, it is possible to use numerical or quantitative data within a naturalistic study to clarify emerging perspectives.

objective of this part of the research? How can I attain that purpose, and what type of methods should I use to achieve my purposes?" Answers to these questions help us assess the nature of the information we require, and the appropriate research tools we therefore apply.

GAINING INSIGHT: MEANING, INTERPRETATION, AND QUALITATIVE RESEARCH

The purposeful move for teachers to understand the experience and perspective of their students is informed by a philosophical standpoint called *phenomenology* that explores the subjective dimensions of human experience. Van Manen's perspective on the study of teaching is quite different from the objective, detached viewpoints that dominate much of the research literature. Through a continuing body of work, Van Manen (1979, 1982, 1984, 1988, 1990) focuses on phenomenological approaches to research and teaching that put us subjectively in touch with *people's everyday experience*. He suggests that a phenomenological perspective offers plausible insights that bring us in more direct contact with the world of our students (Van Manen, 1984).

The purpose of research and teaching, according to Van Manen, is not to put us in *command* of our students, but to put us in *touch* with them. The emphasis is on "seeing" or "insight" rather than explanation—revealing the meanings people attach to events they experience, and the way they are connected to their general life-world. To gain phenomenological insight we do not ask "How do these children learn this material?" but rather "What is the nature of the children's experience of learning?" with the intent of better understanding what the learning experience is like for the children (Van Manen, 1984).

Van Manen's perspective should not be taken as a prescription for the totality of all classroom interaction or all research, since it will sometimes be appropriate for teachers and researchers to stand back and observe the situation objectively, assessing and evaluating events in an unemotional and disengaged manner. At other times educators need to enter the life-world of students to understand how to construct educational activities that are truly meaningful and worthwhile within their everyday lives. Naturalistic inquiry, or qualitative research, provides the tools for these tasks.

A central feature of naturalistic inquiry is that it provides the means for researchers to gain these types of insight by viewing events through a lens of understanding quite different from their personal ways of seeing the world. According to Denzin (1989a, 1989b), research requires an act of interpretation that enables a researcher to view social

---

The use of qualitative data does not necessarily constitute qualitative research; nor does the use of quantitative data constitute a quantitative study. The way the data are manipulated and applied to research outcomes provides an indication of the appropriate use of the terminology. Objective studies seeking causal explanations and generalizable results are appropriately named quantitative or positivistic research, while interpretive studies resulting in detailed and descriptive accounts of people's subjective experience are appropriately identified as naturalistic or qualitative research.

While we can mix methods and data, it is difficult to mix research paradigms within the same study without damaging the utility and integrity of the research. Studies without a random sample, for instance, cannot generalize results. Similarly, qualitative studies that measure fixed variables limit the extent of experiential insight that emerges from naturalistic inquiry.

life from the perspective of another person. This interpretive approach to investigation provides the means to understand how others construct their lives in an ongoing way according to meanings and taken-for-granted procedures that are embedded in the everyday practices of the worlds in which they live.

Denzin suggests that the problem with many human services is that programs, policies, and practices are based on interpretations and judgments of people responsible for their development and delivery. In schools, for instance, faulty or incorrect understandings arise when teachers mistake their own experiences and perspectives for their students' experiences and perspectives. A consequence of this dynamic, then, is that teaching doesn't work adequately because the teaching/learning strategies bear little relationship to the students' meanings, interpretations, and experiences.

Denzin's take on interpretation suggests that far more is involved than "theorizing" about another person's experience. It is an essentially phenomenological[2] process, requiring one to enter into or take the point of view of another's experience; in Mead's (1934) words, "taking the attitude of the other," or in Berger and Luckmann's (1967) terms, entering their "consciousness of everyday life." Understanding, in an interpretive sense, enables us to project ourselves (enter) into the experience of "the other," to understand what they think and feel about particular acts and events. As Denzin says (1989b), "the goal of interpretation is to build true, authentic understandings of the phenomena under investigation" (p. 123). More particularly, though, it seeks to reveal how significant experiences are embedded in the taken-for-granted world of everyday life. Interpretive investigation records the agonies, pains, tragedies, triumphs, and deeply felt emotions—love, pride, dignity, honor, hate, and envy—that influence people's lives.

This perspective has direct implications for teaching. If we consider teaching to be the transmission of objective knowledge, then knowing something of a student's life-world will be peripherally relevant to the task of teaching. Where it is engaged as a process of socially constructed knowledge, it becomes a process of assisting learners to make sense of the material being learned from within their own frames of reference. If we cannot frame our teaching/learning processes in ways enabling diverse learners to understand what they are learning in ways that are meaningful within their own social and cultural life-worlds, then we run the risk of engaging in a series of mechanistic or ritualistic acts that we impose on our students by means of systems of rewards and punishments.

The need to understand the world of classroom and school in these ways has resulted in a proliferation of naturalistic investigation, so that the literature on qualitative research is now both extensive and diverse. Some recent useful contributions, largely focusing on education, include Creswell (2002), De Marrais (1998), Weis and Fine (2000), De Laine (2000), Merchant and Willis (2001), Marshall and Rossman (1999), Silverman (2000), Connelly and Clandinin (1999), and Bogdan and Biklen (1992).

Qualitative, interpretive approaches to inquiry, therefore, provide the principal means for enabling teachers to engage action research to devise teaching and learning strategies more attuned to the realities of students' lives. While it is useful in some contexts to think of students in objective terms, to plan strategies and interventions that enable good learning processes to occur, there will be times when the collaborative construction of learning

---

[2]Phenomenology is the study of phenomena, or ordinary occurrences.

processes or the formulation of socially and culturally appropriate curricula will be enhanced by processes.

When I first entered teaching I was the sole arbiter of the content and processes of teaching in my classroom. I formulated the syllabus from a preordained state curriculum, establishing teaching/learning processes that I had learned in my professional preparation as providing the greatest likelihood of successful learning, and ensured that I maintained sound classroom management processes in order to ensure that students in my class worked systematically.

As a result of my experiences in many different cultural contexts, my preparation for classes and my teaching is much more flexible and participatory. I engage my students in the process of assisting me to formulate a syllabus and, in the process, try to accommodate the diverse backgrounds and learning styles with which they come to my classes. That doesn't mean that I do not prepare thoroughly, or that classroom management is never an issue, but preparation and management have necessarily become a collaborative process. At first, as I learned how to do this, it seemed like extra work, but having become more skilled I can now accomplish it easily. Further, I've learned that by engaging students in these processes they not only become more interested and enthusiastic about their learning, but have some wonderful ideas about both the content and the processes of learning.

While I still appreciate and make use of the information acquired from my studies of educational psychology, sociology, and anthropology—much of it gained through experimental or quasi-experimental research—I am able to place that alongside the knowledge I acquire of my students' experience using naturalistic techniques of inquiry. Each has its place. Each provides tools for acquiring knowledge.

RESEARCH RELATIONSHIPS IN CLASSROOMS AND SCHOOLS

Traditional approaches to experimental research place a strong emphasis on the need for researchers to remain objective, working at an emotional distance and interacting as little as possible with research subjects and the context. In technical terms, action research participants are *positioned* quite differently, taking different roles and having different sets of responsibility within the research act. Teacher researchers are no longer seen as having sole responsibility for enacting the routines of investigation, but act more like team leaders, coordinators, or facilitators. Their role is not to engage in research, but to assist students and other participants to carry out an investigation. In the most ideal version of action research, teachers and students together, sometimes in conjunction with other participants, do the work of clarifying the issue, acquiring information, analyzing the data, constructing reports, and formulating actions.

The importance of this issue, broadly speaking, is that a set of *relationships* has been built into professional life that sometimes needs to be modified in order to carry out an effective action research process. A common assumption built into interactions between professionals and their client groups says, in effect, "I'm the expert here. I know what needs to be done." The assumption here is that training and experience have provided professionals with special knowledge enabling them to make definitive judgments about the nature of the problem experienced and to formulate appropriate solutions to the problem. While this works in some instances, or in instances where the clients are culturally and socially similar to the professional, there are many, many instances where the "expert" knowledge of the professional does not provide the basis for an effective solution to the problem.

Interpretive action research, therefore, starts from quite a different position. It says, in effect, "Although I have professional knowledge that may be useful in exploring the issue or problem facing us, my knowledge is incomplete. We will need to investigate the issue further to reveal other relevant (cultural) knowledge that may extend our understanding of the issue." The teacher's expert knowledge, in this case, becomes another resource to be applied to the issue investigated, and complements the knowledge and understandings of students and parents, whose extended understanding of their own circumstances provides knowledge resources that might usefully be applied to the solution of classroom problems. As anthropologist George Marcus (1998) indicated "[social] affiliations and identities give [research participants] an immense advantage in shaping research. . . . There is . . . a well of life experience that are great assets for achieving the sort of depth [of understanding] that anthropologists have always hoped for from one- to two-year fieldwork projects."

Shelia Baldwin describes the change in relationships that occurred when she, as teacher, became facilitator of her high school students' ethnographic research. "Throughout our time together, I likened our project to a journey we were taking together to discover our community and school culture." One student commented, "I really like that word 'ethnographer.' It makes me feel special." As Shelia indicates, there is some uncertainty at the beginning of the project as students learn that there is not one "correct" answer to the research question. She was eventually surprised, however, at the level of commitment of her students, and realized that she could have established higher degrees of trust and lesser degrees of control from the earliest stages of the study. Her students demonstrated their commitment by attending meetings outside of class hours, turning up at 7:00 A.M. and staying with the project to the end. She ends by saying "They have given me the confidence I needed to be a facilitator [of research]. Now I can allow my students to take ownership."

Many teachers have had similar experiences. One group (Stringer & colleagues, 1997) spoke of the ways in which a participatory approach to research had enhanced their understanding of teaching. "We discovered that teaching is a complex art that requires teachers to facilitate learning, to enact or model what is to be learned, and to create appropriate organizational and social conditions that enable learning to occur . . . engaging students in learning processes that not only enable them to acquire discrete pieces of information, but also to engage in active inquiry and discovery that lead [them] to see and understand their real-life experiences in new ways." The end product is students who take ownership and responsibility for their own learning, and teachers who are able to engender these feelings. One teacher wrote of her experience doing research with other teachers and some of her students (Petty, 1997):

We're much more aware. We're not so definite or absolute anymore in who we are—in a productive way. We're able to absorb so much more when we don't deflect what comes our way. We went through a process of evolution . . . went in with preconceived notions of school, but became aware of different life perspectives and realities. We started from one point, became different people, and have continued to evolve as we tried to recreate the learning experience. We're different teachers for it.

THE SOCIAL PRINCIPLES OF ACTION RESEARCH: NOT JUST A TECHNICAL ROUTINE

There are, however, deeper issues to be considered in engaging participatory action research as a mode of inquiry. Modern social life, with its tendency toward centralized, bureaucratic forms of organization, too easily slides into a form of autocratic operation at odds with the democratic intent of its institutions. Too often, powerful figures in school contexts take on the manner and style of a dictator, imposing their perspectives and agendas on others, and disregarding the needs and views of others. Though this sometimes "works"—the father-figure principal who keeps an iron hand on the reins of the school, or the demanding, disciplinary teacher who will not accept poor behavior or performance—it provides poor socialization for life in a democratic society. Too often people accept the unacceptable, are passive contributors to processes that inhibit or sometimes damage their lives or the lives of their children.

Participatory action research therefore enacts systematic inquiry in ways that are:

- Democratic
- Participatory
- Empowering
- Life-enhancing

These changes highlight the nature and exciting potentials of action research, providing opportunities for teachers, principals, students, and parents to engage in exciting and sometimes exhilarating work together. Processes of investigation, therefore, not only provide information and understanding as key outcomes of a process of inquiry, but provide the possibility of enabling people to develop a sense of togetherness, providing the basis for effective and productive relationships spilling over into all aspects of their lives together. As they participate in action research, people develop high degrees of motivation and are often empowered to act in ways they never thought possible. Action research is not only empowering, therefore, but provides the basis for building democratic learning communities that enhance the environments of schools and institutions.

Recently I engaged in an action research process in a school in a poorer part of town. When debriefing parent participants in the latter stages of the process, I was struck by the excitement evident in their lively talk, shining eyes, and the enthusiasm with which they reviewed their experience. "You know, Ernie," said one, "It was such an empowering experience for us." Asked how it had been empowering, she responded, "Because we were able to do it ourselves, instead of having experts come and do it and tell us. We learned so much in the process, and now we know how to do research." She and another woman who participated in the project indicated a desire to extend their understanding of research processes and to extend their skills. Enrolled as extension students, they sat in on my graduate research class, participating actively and providing class participants with great insight into effective ways of practicing action research in community contexts.

This is not an isolated instance, as I've shared the excitement and experienced the feelings of accomplishment of young children, teenagers, teachers, principals, parents, student teachers, graduate students, and professors in large cities, small country towns, and remote communities. My experience encompasses a wide range of social and cultural contexts on two continents, and the power of participatory processes to engage enthusiasm and excitement still excites me. For me, action research is not a dreary, objective, mechanistic process, but a vital, energizing process that engages the mind, enhances the spirit, and creates the unity that enables people to accomplish highly significant goals. At its best, it is a transformational experience enabling people to see the world anew, and in some cases, to literally change their lives.

There is another side to action research, however, that continues to sustain me professionally: the ability to provide the means to accomplish exciting work in the most difficult of circumstances. In a world made increasingly by the forces of economic rationalism and accountability, where every activity must be justified in terms of a pre-specified "benchmark" and justified in dollar terms, the spiritual and artistic side of education can easily be lost in a maze of technical, mechanistic, and clinical procedures that too easily dulls and nullifies the creative, life-enhancing outcomes of a truly educational experience. The energy and excitement generated by collaborative accomplishment not only provides the means to accomplish the technical, clinical goals of our work, but to do so in ways that are truly meaningful and enriching.

The process of collaboratively working toward that goal not only provides a wide range of expertise, both professional and cultural, but also generates positive working relationships. By including students and parents in the search for solutions to these types of problems we open the possibility of making use of their wisdom, and acknowledging the concrete realities affecting student behavior and performance. Moreover, by engaging them in processes of inquiry that recognize their competence and worth, we provide the basis for developing productive relationships that engender trust and understanding. Even the poorest communities have a store of experience and local knowledge that can be incorporated into exciting and meaningful activities that have the power to transform the education of people and children.

This participatory approach to research therefore accomplishes both a sense of community and a living democracy. It provides the means to bring people together in dialogic and productive relationships, enabling the development of a sense of community through the sharing of perspectives, the negotiation of meaning, and the production of collaboratively produced activities, programs, and projects. The search for harmony, peace, caring, and joy can be integrated with technical efficiency in ways that create truly democratic and humane classrooms and schools.

CONCLUSION

Research texts quite often work on an unspoken assumption that applications of the technical routines of scientific research provide the basis for enlightened and improved professional practice. This chapter has suggested the need to broaden ideas about the nature and function of research to ensure that they acknowledge and take into account the social and human dimensions of educational life. While scientifically validated knowledge truly has the potential to increase understanding of significant features of our social life and educational practice, to the extent that it fails to acknowledge or take into account the social, cultural, ethical, and political nature of social life, it fails to provide the means to improve people's educational endeavors.

The participatory and interpretive approach to action research found in this text seeks to provide a more balanced approach to inquiry, providing research procedures that are conducive of democratic and humane social processes within classrooms and schools. The intent is to provide a rigorous approach to inquiry that legitimizes the perspectives and experiences of all people involved, takes account of scientifically validated information in the processes, and encompasses the means for accomplishing sustainable and effective educational practices that really make a difference in people's lives.

Technical routines of research are accomplished within a set of principles that values the human dimensions of educational life.

SUMMARY

Understanding Action Research: Exploring Issues of Paradigm and Method

The chapter distinguishes between two major research paradigms: *Objective science*, sometimes called scientific positivism, and *naturalistic inquiry*, often referred to as qualitative or interpretive research.

Objective science assumes a fixed universe that can be observed and explained with precision. Through the experimental method it seeks generalizable information with high degrees of reliability that can be applied across diverse settings. It seeks high degrees of predictability and control of events.

Naturalistic inquiry focuses on understanding the way people interpret events in their everyday lives. It makes use of qualitative methods that use both qualitative and quantitative information to gain insight and understanding of issues and events.

Action research requires a different set of relationships than those often engaged by professionals. It seeks to make use of the deep-seated and extended understandings people have of their own situations and their own experiences.

Action research embodies a set of social principles that are both democratic and ethical. It seeks to engage processes of inquiry that are democratic, participatory, empowering, and life enhancing.

Initiating a Study:
Research Design

From Chapter 3 of *Action Research in Education*, Second Edition. Ernie Stringer. Copyright © 2008 by Pearson Education, Inc. All rights reserved.

Initiating a Study: Research Design

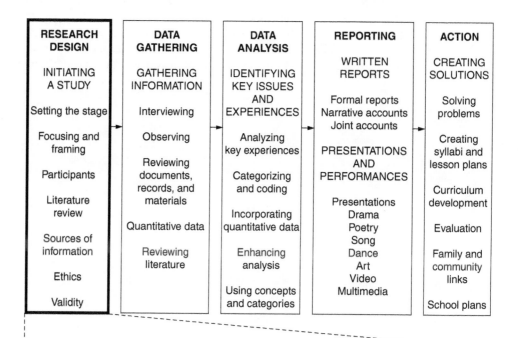

RESEARCH DESIGN	DATA GATHERING	DATA ANALYSIS	REPORTING	ACTION
INITIATING A STUDY	GATHERING INFORMATION	IDENTIFYING KEY ISSUES AND EXPERIENCES	WRITTEN REPORTS	CREATING SOLUTIONS
Setting the stage	Interviewing	Analyzing key experiences	Formal reports Narrative accounts Joint accounts	Solving problems
Focusing and framing	Observing	Categorizing and coding	PRESENTATIONS AND PERFORMANCES	Creating syllabi and lesson plans
Participants	Reviewing documents, records, and materials	Incorporating quantitative data	Presentations Drama Poetry	Curriculum development
Literature review	Quantitative data	Enhancing analysis	Song Dance Art	Evaluation
Sources of information	Reviewing literature	Using concepts and categories	Video Multimedia	Family and community links
Ethics				School plans
Validity				

Contents of the Chapter

This chapter presents ways of initiating a research study. It describes procedures for:

1. creating a productive research environment.
2. *designing* the study, that is, formulating an action plan for the research processes.
3. *focusing* the study and stating it in researchable terms.
4. *framing* the scope of the inquiry.
5. engaging in a preliminary *review of the literature.*
6. identifying *sources of data.*
7. describing methods of *data analysis.*
8. taking account of *ethical* considerations.
9. establishing the validity of the study.

SETTING THE STAGE: CREATING A PRODUCTIVE RESEARCH ENVIRONMENT

Action research provides the means for teachers and administrators to use systematic processes of inquiry to enrich and enhance the planning and operation of the routine tasks of schooling—planning, evaluation, problem solving, and so on. This chapter sets out the preliminary processes that enable you to incorporate a clear plan to integrate a process of inquiry into regular school teaching and administrative practices.

Technical routines, however, are only part of the picture, and to the extent that they have an effect on other people—students, colleagues, administrators, parents—they must necessarily be enacted with the dignity and kindness that befits any civilized social activity. In the sections that follow, therefore, the technical features of designing an effective action research process are presented, and are complemented by working principles that focus on the human dimensions of classroom and school life. Effective action research is a holistic process that takes into account *all* features and elements of a situation likely to have an effect on the issue investigated. Since the process is as important as the product, we start by focusing on features of the research context that need to be taken into account in developing positive working environments that form the basis for effective action.

WITH HEAD, HEART, AND HAND: THE HUMAN DIMENSIONS OF ACTION RESEARCH

When we can work with head, heart and hand, we begin to shape a kind of community that is responsive to many different communities, in different places and in different times, and one that opens many ways forward. (Kelly & Sewell, 1988)

Too often students move through routinized reading and writing tasks, engaging their hands, and to some extent their heads, but without having their hearts in it. Teachers may likewise move mechanically through a teaching routine, maintaining order in their classes as they "keep the kids quiet" and "cover the content of the curriculum," their hearts likewise disengaged. In such circumstances classroom life threatens to become tedious, boring, and irrelevant, to be endured by students to gain a class credit, certificate, or diploma. Good teaching provides learning experiences that excite students and provide knowledge and skills that enhance their lives. One of the very productive aspects of both teaching and research is the ability to fully engage all dimensions of experience, to employ the heads, hands, and hearts of the people who participate in classroom and school.

This is not always an easy task, as teachers often face groups of students who are disinterested, fractious, or rebellious. One of the enduring tasks of teaching is to develop and sustain student interest, and experienced teachers engage a broad repertoire of strategies with this end in mind. We speak of the need to "motivate" students as part of the language of instruction, often attributing student disinterest to personality factors such as poor self-concept or poor concentration, or to a student's home or community background. Motivation is often seen as extrinsic to the content of learning, so that grades, assessments, or reward systems become primary means for encouraging students to maintain their focus and/or interest in their work. Motivation, however, may be more broadly conceived as engaging the *heart*, or the *spirit*, of the students and others with whom we work, so they do not just "go through the motions," but take ownership for their work and engage it joyously, enthusiastically, and creatively. The same is true for teachers themselves, who must constantly find ways to develop and sustain the creative energy required for their demanding day-to-day work with children in schools.

Teachers sometimes have difficulty imagining that research could make such a difference in their classroom lives. As a teacher myself, I discovered the energy emerging from participatory processes of inquiry. Over the past decades, however, I have been humbled by the sometimes impassioned comments of ordinary teachers who have embraced these tenets. Often working in the most difficult of situations, they have been able to transform their classroom and teaching lives, engaging creative energies of students, families, and community people. One preschool teacher, engaging this form of research for the first time, commented "It has been a long time since I have had a paradigmatic shift like this in such a profound way. [It] is like a small earthquake or miniature shock of lightening arousing me from my day-to-day, automatic pilot semi-slumber." These types of responses from people with whom I work in school and community settings continue to sustain my excitement and enthusiasm. The technical routines I learn and teach are important, but the process by which they become instilled in people's experience is a central ingredient of a truly educational experience. When I teach I still aspire to a productive and enjoyable classroom experience for my students and myself. After decades in the classroom I can still accomplish this, most times, in most places.

One of the problems of engaging the "heart" of our students, however, lies in the complexity teachers face in their daily class lives. My work alongside Australian Aboriginal people, whose needs are often quite different from the mainstream population, has sensitized me to this facet of school life. These experiences have been reinforced by my work in American schools and universities, where African American, Hispanic, Native American, and other groups of students provide a rich tapestry of humanity that not only holds a fertile cultural resource, but challenges teachers to accommodate the diversity that exists in their classrooms. Often the complexity of these situations encourages us to ignore the implicit differences in students, speaking of them in technical or objectifying language—"organisms," "the learner," or "the student," and characterizing their failure to accomplish learning objectives in terms of "deviance" or other personal inadequacies. We often focus on "interventions" or "strategies" to repair their inappropriate or inadequate performances without acknowledging the possibility of engaging the resourcefulness of the students with whom we work.

The approach to action research presented in this text works on the assumption that people, even very young people, have deep and extended understandings of their lives, enabling them to negotiate their ways through an often bewildering and unpredictable lifeworld. It is our willingness to acknowledge the legitimacy of their worldviews, and the wisdom that enables them to survive and sometimes thrive in difficult circumstances, that is at the heart of the participatory processes described in this text. The use of interviews as a central component of action research enables us to listen carefully to what people say, to record and represent events in their own terms, and to use their perceptions and interpretations in formulating plans and activities. The task is not to convince them of the inadequacies of their perspective, but to find ways of enabling them, through sharing each other's perspectives, to formulate more productive understandings of their own situation.

This orientation to research therefore seeks to enhance people's feelings of competence and worth, engaging them in processes that provide an affirmation of themselves, their friends, their families, and their communities. Our work with others—students, colleagues, parents, and administrators—enables them to maintain a constructive vision of themselves, anchoring them in a productive perspective of their worlds and enabling them to work easily and comfortably with those around them. Engaging the heart means caring, in an ongoing way, about those facets of human experience that make a difference in the quality of their day-to-day lives. When we talk of the "heart" of the matter, or engaging the heart of the people, we are talking of their feelings of pride, dignity, identity, responsibility, and locatedness (see Figure 1).

| **Pride** |
| Feelings of personal worth |
| **Dignity** |
| Feelings of competence |
| **Identity** |
| Acknowledging the worth of social identities: female, mother, person-of-color, parent, etc. |
| **Responsibility** |
| Acknowledging their ability to be responsible for their actions |
| **Space** |
| Feelings of comfort that result from working in nonthreatening physical environments |
| **Place** |
| Feelings of having a legitimate place in the social context |

Figure 1
The Human Dimensions of Action Research

The energy and joy emerging from research processes that hear the voices of the people, engage their knowledge and skills, and enable them to actively participate in the construction of activities, events, projects, programs, and services have been an integral part of my professional experience for many years. When I see people talk with shining eyes of their accomplishments, when I see them deeply engaged in work affecting their lives, when I see them moved to upgrade and extend their education, and continue to move in often-difficult terrain over extended periods, I know that their hearts have been engaged. They rarely do so in isolation, however; the work they accomplish is enhanced by the common unity they share with those with whom they have worked.

WORKING PRINCIPLES OF ACTION RESEARCH

In another publication (Stringer, 2007a), I present a group of key concepts holding the principles of action research. The first key principle is that of *relationship*, for when relationships are wrong, it is hard to accomplish the desired outcomes of any project. *Communication* also is a central feature of action research, enabling all participants to remain informed of and in harmony with the different activities in which people are engaged. The principle of *inclusion* speaks to the need to ensure that all people whose lives are affected or who have an effect on the issue investigated are included, and that all significant factors having an effect are taken into account. Finally, the principle of *participation* signals the need to ensure that people are actively engaged in the work of the project, gaining energy from the resulting feelings of ownership and accomplishment.

As we learn the technical aspects of research, we also need to encompass and integrate behaviors and interactional styles that facilitate the work we wish to accomplish. We need to take account, therefore, of the following features of our work in all that we do.

Relationships

Good working relationships enable individuals and groups to trust each other, provide high levels of motivation, and provide the basis for continuing research activities over the sometimes long periods required to deal with significant issues. Good working relationships:

- promote feelings of equality for all people involved.
- maintain harmony.
- avoid conflicts, where possible.
- resolve conflicts that arise, openly and dialogically.
- accept people as they are, not as some people think they ought to be.
- encourage personal, cooperative relationships, rather than impersonal, competitive, conflictual, or authoritarian relationships.
- are sensitive to people's feelings.

Communication

Maintaining good relationships depends, to a significant extent, on the ability of people to communicate effectively. The quality, consistency, and correctness of communication have a vital effect on interactions between individuals and groups. Their work together is likely to be short-lived or ineffectual if people talk to each other in disparaging or demeaning ways, if they fail to provide information about their activities, or if they distort or selectively communicate information.

Effective communication occurs when all participants:

- listen attentively to each other.
- accept and act upon what is said.
- can understand what has been said.
- are truthful and sincere.
- act in socially and culturally appropriate ways.
- regularly advise others about what is happening.

Participation

It is normal practice for professional practitioners to take responsibility for all that needs to be done in their sphere of operation. They either do things themselves or engage someone to do it for them. While this is quite necessary for many activities related to schooling and other professional areas, one of the purposes of action research is to engage the natural expertise and experience of all participants. When people are able to see that their worth is acknowledged by the activities in which they are able to engage, high levels of personal investment—of resources, time, and emotion—often result. Active participation is very empowering, especially for people who have a poor self-image. Another of the key features of action research, therefore, is for facilitators to provide opportunities for people to demonstrate their competence by engaging in research-related activities themselves. Sometimes people may commence with quite simple tasks, taking on increasingly complex activities as their confidence increases. Although this sometimes requires more time and considerable patience on the part of research facilitators, the long-term benefits easily outweigh the initial outlay of time and effort.

Participation is most effective when it:

- enables significant levels of active involvement.
- enables people to perform significant tasks.
- provides support for people as they learn to act for themselves.
- encourages plans and activities that people are able to accomplish themselves.
- deals personally with people rather than with their representatives or agents.

Inclusion

Often people are tempted to carve out a piece of "territory," or to "take charge" of an issue. In professional life, teachers and administrators almost automatically take responsibility for any actions required to deal with issues within their professional realm. Further, there is often pressure to find short-term solutions to complex problems with a long history, providing teachers and/or administrators with the temptation to take immediate action themselves. Usually, these actions fail to take into account many of the factors contributing to the problem or to include people who are an integral part of the context or whose lives are substantially affected by the problem.

Inclusion requires participants to:

- involve all relevant groups and individuals whose lives are affected by the issue investigated.
- take account of all relevant issues affecting the research question.
- cooperate with related groups, agencies, and organizations where necessary.
- ensure all relevant groups benefit from activities.

RESEARCH DESIGN

As teacher researchers engage in action research, they need to have a clear view of the details of the investigation in which they will be engaged. Initially they will construct a preliminary picture of the project, but will work with other stakeholders to refine this picture and incorporate more details of research activities.

As they commence the work of inquiry they will design the research, detailing an action plan listing the steps to be taken. The design will include:

- **Building a preliminary picture:** Identifying the research problem and the people affected by or having an effect on the problem.
- **Focusing:** Refining the statement of the research problem, the research question, and the research objectives.
- **Framing:** Establishing the scope of the inquiry.
- **Sampling:** Determining procedures for identifying project participants.
- **Sources of information/data:** Identifying stakeholding groups, sites and settings, statistical records, and other sources of documentary information providing input to the study.
- **Form of the information/data:** Determining the type of information that will inform the inquiry—interview transcripts, observational records, review summaries, televisual documentaries, formal research reports, school records, and so on.
- **Data gathering procedures:** Determining how information will be gathered—including interviews, focus groups, observations, review of materials and equipment, and so on.
- **Data analysis procedures:** Selecting methods of distilling information to identify key features, concepts, or meanings—for example, event analysis, categorizing, and coding.
- **Ethics:** Taking steps to ensure that no harm is done to people through their inclusion in the research.
- **Validity:** Establishing procedures used to enhance the strength of the research.

BUILDING A PRELIMINARY PICTURE: THE REFLECTIVE PRACTITIONER

One of the first difficulties confronting researchers is to acquire clarity about the nature and purposes of the research. In their day-to-day work, teachers deal with a vast array of interrelated issues and problems that have a continuing impact on their students' learning. The initial processes of designing an action research study can be assisted by implementing a simple process of reflection—depicted here as a "look-think-act" sequence—that enables the teacher researcher to build a clear picture of the issue on which the research is focused, and the context in which it will be played out. In the first research cycle, teacher researchers carefully observe relevant classroom or school settings and then reflect on their observations to clarify the nature of the research problem. They identify the people who will be involved and formulate the research question upon which the study will initially focus. Continuing cycles of the look-think-act process enable the teacher researcher and other participants to further refine these details as they explore the issue.

For example, a teacher may not be happy with what her students are accomplishing in an area of study, and thus may ask the question "How can I improve student learning of [content area] in my classroom?" To answer this question effectively she will need to reflect on the range of issues that may be influencing her students' performance. She will "look" at the students in her classroom, the classroom itself, and the way she has organized learning in this area. As she does so, she will "think," reflecting on the means by which she can identify the source of the problem—poor student performance. Finally, she will "act," planning a process of systematic inquiry that will lead to more effective teaching/learning processes that accomplish her desired end.

In general terms, the look-think-act routine mirrors a traditional research process—look = gathering data; think = analyzing data; act = reporting results (see Figure 2). In the first phase of action research:

Look entails gathering information to build a preliminary picture of the situation, enabling the researcher to describe *who* is involved; *what* is happening; and *how, where,* and *when* events and activities occur. Information is acquired by observing participants, the context, and identifying factors influencing the issue to be investigated.

Think requires researchers to reflect on the emerging picture. It is essentially preliminary analysis of the situation that enables researchers to develop a clearer understanding of

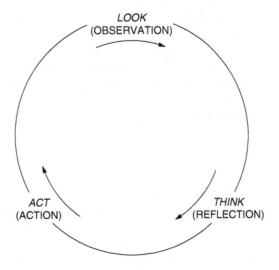

Figure 2
The Look-Think-Act Research Cycle

what is happening, how it is happening, and the stakeholding groups affected by or affecting the issue.

Act defines the actions emerging from reflection. It requires people to *plan* their next steps and *implement* appropriate activity. *Evaluation* of these steps requires another cycle of the look-think-act process.

FOCUSING THE STUDY

In the everyday world of the classroom, teachers are confronted with an ongoing series of small crises and problems that they solve using a repertoire of skills and knowledge acquired through their professional training and school experience. More systematic research becomes necessary when they find themselves unable to find an effective solution to a persistent or serious problem. Identifying the point of entry is sometimes not easy, since any problems tend to occur as an interrelated or intertwined series of events or features of a situation. Behavioral problems are often associated with poor academic performance, negative attitudes, lack of engagement, and so on. Trying to define what *the problem* is can easily become a "chicken-and-egg" process having no particular beginning or end, or no clearly defined cause-and-effect relationships.

Sometimes our first analysis of a situation focuses on related events that prove to be peripheral to the problem about which we are concerned. A recent meeting of a school board I attended focused on the "problem" of lack of parent participation, with members discussing ways of increasing parent participation. Eventually I asked board members whether, in fact, parent participation was the "real" problem, and asked them to consider "the problem behind the problem." They spoke of a number of issues about which they were concerned, including the failure of parents to engage in required actions to remediate their children's poor academic performance or inappropriate behavior. In this case, the "problem" upon which the school board initially focused turned out to be multidimensional, parent participation being one facet of more deep-seated educational problems. Once the underlying problems were identified, the board was able to reflect more broadly on the issues about which they were concerned. The "problem" of parent participation turned out to be a suggested solution that was not working. In the first stages of research, therefore, research participants need to carefully reflect on the nature of "the problem" about which they are concerned.

One of the major strengths of qualitative research is its ability to allow researchers to tentatively state the problem, then refine and reframe the study by continuing iterations of the look-think-act research cycle. In one study, for instance, researchers focused initially on afterschool vandalism in the local district and attributed it to poor parental supervision. Preliminary investigations revealed, however, that youth from their school suffered from boredom and frustration because of the lack of activities or facilities in their small town. The investigation took a markedly different turn at this point, focusing more clearly on exactly what facilities were available, and what might be developed. In another investigation, preliminary inquiries indicated to a classroom teacher that an apparent lack of interest in reading in her class could be attributed more clearly to her teaching methods and the reading material she used. She refocused her research at this point from her students to her own syllabus.

At this stage the research is essentially a reflective process, requiring research participants to think carefully through all dimensions of the issue causing concern. The first step is to reflect carefully on what is happening that is problematic and what issues and events are related to that problem. To focus the research more clearly, the issue or problem is stated in the form of a researchable question, and the objective of studying that issue is identified. The following should be clearly stated:[1]

- The **issue or topic** to be studied: Define which issues or events are causing concern.
- The **research problem:** State the issue as a problem.
- The **research question:** Reframe that problem as a question—asking, in effect, "What is happening here?"
- The **research objective:** Describe what we would hope to achieve by studying this question.[2]

The preliminary reflective process for developing the focus of the study is assisted by dialogue with both potential participants and colleagues. While it is possible that the research focus may later change as other participants pose their own particular questions, the initiator of the project should be clear about his or her own research questions and their significance.

The initial development of the research question should focus on *how* participants and other stakeholders experience the problematic issue and *how* they interpret events and other information. How is it that these problems occur? How do students perceive that they manage to complete their assignments? How do students describe learning processes that

---

Shelley Jones's study of reading in her class was defined in the following terms:

Issue: Students are consistently failing to complete their reading homework, are listless in reading lessons, and score poorly on reading proficiency tests.
Problem: The students are uninterested in reading.
Question: How do students experience reading?
Objective: To understand what the experience of reading means to students.

---

[1] Since this is a qualitative research study, a research hypothesis—a suggested answer to the research question—is not part of the design. Qualitative or interpretive inquiry is hypothesis generating, rather than hypothesis testing. "Testing" of the "answers" generated by an action research process is accomplished through continual cycling through the look-think-act routine, so that actions put into place as a result of the first cycle of investigation are subject to evaluative processes through further observation and analysis—looking and thinking.
[2] Qualitative studies usually focus on *understanding* people's experience and perspectives as a common outcome of the research process. Quantitative or experimental studies, on the other hand, more often focus on *causal explanations* that explain how one group of variables is "caused" by the effect of preceding variables.

are stimulating? In action research the focus is largely on events and their interpretation, rather than factual information or strongly developed causal connections explaining "why" events occur.

By developing a clear, precise, and focused research question, researchers add an essential reference point into their inquiry. Once investigations have commenced, they are able to evaluate the emerging data according to its reference to the research question. The initial research question should be shared by all participants and reiterated consistently throughout the research cycles as a constant guide to investigation.

FRAMING THE STUDY: DELIMITING THE SCOPE OF THE INQUIRY

As research participants identify and clarify the research issues and questions, they will also need to define the broad parameters of the study, determining whether it will be limited in scope, involving a small number of people over a small time period, or whether more extended study is required. Sometimes it is a relatively simple matter to work with students within a classroom to formulate successful strategies to solve the problem studied. At other times it may be necessary to work in conjunction with teachers from other classes, with the school administration, and/or with families. Before commencing research, therefore, participants will make decisions about the sample of people to be included in the study, the sites or settings in which the research will take place, and the times the research activities will take place. Decisions will also be made about the extent of participation by those involved in the study, defining who will be involved in the various research activities and who will monitor and support people in their research work.

These considerations run hand-in-hand with the need to consider the breadth of issues to be incorporated into the study. Including too many issues is likely to make the study complex and unwieldy, but delimiting the study too closely may neglect issues that have an important bearing on the problem. In the Barrios Juntos study, for instance, participants concerned with ways of improving parent participation in the school decided to focus their study on parent–teacher conferences, rather than investigating the other possible forums and vehicles of parent participation. In this instance, the research revealed ways in which parent–teacher conferences could be improved, but also identified a range of related issues that would need to be addressed. Researchers therefore will initially broadly identify:

- **What:** What is the problem requiring investigation? What is my central research question?
- **Participants:** *Who* are the stakeholders? Which people are affected by or have an effect on the issue being studied? Students? Teachers? Administrators? Parents or other family members? Others?
- **Place:** *Where* will the research take place? Which sites or settings will be included in the study? Classrooms? Schoolyard? Offices? Homes? Other locations?
- **Time:** *When* will the research begin? How long might it take?
- **Scope:** What is the likely scope of the issues to be investigated? Student academic experience? Student reading experience? Reading comprehension experience?

Student experiences of the curriculum, classroom, or learning? Student and teacher experiences of school organization? Student, teacher, and parent perspectives on student experiences?

Once the research participants have clarified the focus, frame, and scope of the research, they will undertake a preliminary review of the literature to identify other perspectives on the issue embedded in the literature. This may assist them to further clarify the nature and extent of their investigations.

Preliminary Literature Review

As Creswell (2002) points out, literature reviews for qualitative research have different purposes than those in quantitative research. While substantial use of the literature provides the basis for formulating a quantitative study, qualitative studies use the literature review quite minimally in the earlier phases of a study. Since the latter focuses on stakeholder experiences and perspectives, preformulation of the issue according to concepts and analyses in the literature is deemed inappropriate at this point. Because of the nature of qualitative research, initial conceptions of the research are always assumed to be provisional, thus limiting the possibility of an exhaustive review of the literature.

Understandings and information emerging from the literature, however, may augment, complement, or challenge stakeholder perspectives as the study progresses. Since classroom and school life have been subjects of study for many decades, research participants may increase the power of their investigation by reviewing literature that speaks to emerging concepts and issues. In some cases they may identify potential solutions to the problem that have been successfully enacted in other contexts, or acquire information that clarifies issues emerging in the study. Frequently, salient issues emerging in the data collection phase influence the direction of the investigation, causing participants to pursue different but related questions. Hence the literature search will evolve as an ongoing feature of the research process, emerging in accordance with the directions and agendas indicated by participant-constructed descriptions of the situation.

Literature Search The first phase of a search requires researchers to identify relevant literature. This task is greatly enhanced by the capabilities of computer-assisted search engines available in most libraries. It will be necessary to identify three or four key concepts related to the issue to feed into the search routine. Where large numbers of items are identified, it may be necessary to delineate further key concepts to narrow the search to the most relevant sources of information. Perusing annotated collections, such as ERIC, which provide a brief description of the content of the reading, may enhance this process.

An increasing body of material is available on the web, providing researchers with useful resources for their study. Sole reliance on the web, however, is not recommended, as the information available from web sources tends to be incomplete and patchy. As in library searches, researchers will need to identify key concepts to feed into the search process.

Researchers often distinguish between:

- **Primary sources** that provide direct reports of original research
- **Secondary sources** that report on or summarize primary source material
- **Professional literature** based on the perspectives of experienced professionals

- **Institutional reports** from government or institutional authorities
- **Practice literature** that presents or advocates particular approaches to professional practice

University and professional libraries provide a wide variety of relevant literature, including theses and dissertations, journals, books, handbooks, abstracts, and encyclopedias. Library staff can often assist in identifying initial reading pertinent to the problem being investigated, but review of any material will identify other sources of information, so that a review of the literature becomes an ever-expanding search. Researchers should note sources cited in journal articles, research reports, and texts, then review those for further information.

Identifying Different Perspectives in the Literature The preliminary literature review extends the think/reflect part of the research cycle, providing new possibilities for conceptualizing or interpreting the issue. The preliminary search therefore should be sufficiently broad to provide researchers with an understanding of the different perspectives and types of information presented within the literature. These will not only differ according to the disciplines of the authors—psychology, sociology, cultural studies, and so on—but also according to different theoretical positions from within each discipline. The literature may also vary according to the formal and informal reports from a variety of educational sources, including school, district, state, and national documents. It may include video/television documentaries, as well as information on projects and activities available on the web.

As the project progresses, participants will select, review, and evaluate relevant literature as part of the processes of data collection, identifying pertinent information to enhance the understandings emerging from other sources. Studies by other people within the literature become other perspectives (or stakeholders) to be incorporated into the process of data collection and analysis. The preliminary review of the literature within the first iteration of the action research cycle is conducted through the lens of the initial research question, alerting participants to other findings about similar problems, assisting with the refinement of the research question, and/or providing insight into research methods.

Sampling: Selecting Participants

In most studies limits on time and resources make it impossible to include all people who might potentially inform the research process, so it is necessary to select a smaller group to provide the information (data) on which the research is grounded. A technique called *purposive*, or *purposeful, sampling* seeks to ensure that the diverse perspectives of people likely to affect the issue are included in the study. Creswell (2002) suggests that purposive sampling seeks to select participants for a variety of purposes. These include:

- people who represent the diverse perspectives found in any social context (maximal variation sampling)
- particularly troublesome or enlightening cases (extreme case sampling)
- participants who are "typical" of people in the setting (typical sampling)
- participants who have particular knowledge related to the issue studied (theory or concept sampling)

In all cases, researchers need to purposively select a sample of participants that represents the variation of perspectives and experiences across all groups and subgroups who affect or are affected by the issue under investigation—the stakeholders in the study.[3]

The first task is to identify the primary stakeholding groups[4]—that is, the groups most centrally involved or affected by the issue studied. If a study is concerned about poorly performing boys in a classroom, the poorly performing boys would be the primary stakeholding group, while a study of parent participation in school would have parents as the primary stakeholders. Sometimes the primary stakeholding groups are complementary groups. A study of a classroom issue might include teachers and students as primary stakeholders, while a study of parent participation might include parents, teachers, and students.

Sometimes the primary stakeholders are able to resolve the problem themselves and there is no need to extend their study further. Where the problem persists, however, research participants need to identify other stakeholders—other people likely to have an effect on the issue studied. Parents, other teachers, or school administrators may need to be included, depending on the nature of the problem investigated. They need to ensure that all relevant groups are included—that girls and boys are represented in their sample, and that students from poorer families as well as those from more middle-class homes are an integral part of the study. Each racial, ethnic, or cultural group should also be included. Depending on the context, it may be necessary for researchers to include members of different social cliques, religious affiliations, sporting groups, or other types of groups represented in the social setting.

While it is not always possible to include people from *all* groups in any setting, those selected should include participants from groups likely to have a significant impact on the issue studied, or to be impacted by that issue. To fail to include participants because it is not convenient, because they show little interest, or because they are noncommunicative is to put the effectiveness of the study at risk. There is a need to establish research relationships to maximize the possibility of including everyone likely to affect the issue studied.

It is not always possible for researchers to nominate in advance those who need to be included in a study. A technique called *snowballing* enables researchers to ask participants who they think needs to be included, or to ask someone they might nominate who has quite a different perspective or set of experiences related to the issue studied. In this way, researchers commence by defining likely participants, but extend their sample to be more inclusive of the diverse and significant perspectives included in the study.

Any group, however, is likely to include people who are natural leaders, or who in some way are able to sway the opinions or perspectives of others in their group—sometimes referred to as opinion leaders. Researchers should try to ensure that the sample selected includes both natural leaders and opinion leaders. A general rule of thumb in this process is to ask "Who can speak for this group? Whose word will group members acknowledge as representing their perspective?"

---

[3]Purposive sampling differs in nature and purpose from the random sampling used for experimental studies. A random sample drawn from a larger population enables experimental researchers to use statistical procedures to generalize from that sample to a larger population. Rather than seeking to generalize, action research seeks solutions to problems and questions that are quite context specific.

[4]In some literature the *primary stakeholding group* is referred to as the *critical reference group*. The intent, however, is similar—to focus on those primarily affected by the issue studied.

The research design may not specify a particular sample, therefore, but will describe the procedures for identifying those who will be active participants in the study.

Sources and Forms of Information (Data Gathering)

In planning the study researchers also need to identify the type of information that will be gathered, and the source of that information. Sources may include interviews with stakeholders—the "sample" described earlier—observation of people, places, events, or activities; materials and equipment; work samples; documents, records, and reports; relevant literature; and so on.

The research design should stipulate the methods employed to access these types of information, including interviews, focus groups, observations, literature and document reviews, photographs, and video and audio recording. Because of the nature of qualitative research it is not possible to signal precisely all sources of information, but the design should provide participants with guidance about where, when, how, and from whom initial information will be acquired. Later iterations of the research may include structured questionnaires, surveys, or other data gathering instruments.

Distilling the Information (Data Analysis)

The research design should inform participants and those reading research proposals of the type of data analysis to be used in the study. The research design should clearly signal the type of data analysis employed and the way in which analyzed data will be used to formulate actions.

RESEARCH DESIGN

A qualitative action research design provides a description of:

1. **Focus:** A statement of the issue, the research problem, the research question, and research objectives.
2. **Framing the scope of inquiry:** The place, the time, the stakeholding groups, and the scope of the issues included in the study.
3. **Preliminary literature review:** Processes for reviewing the literature.
4. **Sources of information/data:** The stakeholders, sites and settings, and literature from which information will be acquired.
5. **Data gathering processes:** Ways information will be gathered—interviews, observation, review of materials and equipment, and so on.
6. **Data analysis processes:** Procedures used for distilling information.

RESEARCH ETHICS

The research design also includes ethical considerations that protect the well-being and interests of research participants. Punch (1994) suggests that "the view that science is intrinsically neutral and essentially beneficial disappeared with the revelations at the

Nuremberg trials." Some well-known studies have shown that researchers are not always aware of potential harm that may come to those who participate in research studies (e.g., Horowitz, 1970; Milgram, 1963). Most public institutions and professional organizations have formal procedures to ensure that researchers do not knowingly or unknowingly put research participants at risk. The research design includes procedures for ensuring the safety of the participants. As Sieber (1992) indicates, sound ethics and sound methodology go hand in hand.

Universities have Internal Review Boards (IRB) to ensure the ethical conduct of research engaged in by students and faculty. Usually such boards require a copy of the proposal, and an indication of the procedures that will ensure the safety of research participants, including the confidentiality of research processes. Although each university will have its own set of rules, the following procedures provide a general means to satisfy most IRB regulations.

Confidentiality, Care, and Sensitivity

When people talk for extended periods they often speak of very private matters, revealing highly problematic events or even potentially harmful information. A prime directive of social research is to protect the anonymity of participants. In practice it is best to assume that *all* information acquired is highly confidential. Where we require information to be shared with other participants or audiences, we must first ask relevant participants for permission to do so. When I read back my field notes, or share analyzed information with participants, I ask "Is there anything here you would not like to reveal to other people in this project?" If they appear unsure, I inform them that it may be possible to present the information, but to disguise its source. We can do this by using fictitious names, or by reporting it generally—"Some people suggest that . . ." or "Other participants provide a different perspective on . . ."

Aligned with confidentiality is the duty of care we have to participants. We need to ensure that information is stored securely so that others do not inadvertently see it. We certainly should not share recorded information with others without permission of the persons concerned, even if that information points to apparently harmful events in a person's life—drug abuse, physical abuse, and so on. This points to another possibility occasionally arising in the processes of extended interview—the recall of distressing events sometimes creates a deep emotional response. Duty of care requires researchers to provide sufficient time for the person to "debrief" by talking through issues or events to a point of comfort, or by putting the individual in contact with a family member or counselor who can assist in resolving the situation.

Permissions

Permission is not usually required when teachers engage in research directly related to their ongoing work in the classroom. Where they engage in more extended studies involving other school staff, children from other classes, or parents, then they may need to obtain formal permission prior to commencing the project. To the extent that the research becomes a public process, therefore, where people's privacy or personal well-being is "at risk," written permission from a person in a position of authority is warranted—a principal, school district superintendent, or other relevant authority. In these circumstances it is necessary to provide information about the nature of the research, the significance of the study, and the ways in which ethical considerations will be taken into account. It is useful to attach a copy of the research design to the request for permission to pursue the study.

Where research is associated with a university course or program, the institution itself will usually have processes for reviewing research through an ethics committee. A similar system operates in school districts. Though the procedures are sometimes unwieldy and time consuming, they provide a means of ensuring that people's privacy is not violated and that research processes do not interfere with their well-being.

Informed Consent

In many contexts, protocols require those facilitating research to engage processes of informed consent. This requires the research facilitator and others engaged in data gathering to:

- Inform each participant of the purpose and nature of the study.
- Ask whether they wish to participate.
- Ask permission to record information they provide.
- Assure them of the confidentiality of that information.
- Advise them that they may withdraw at any stage and have their recorded information returned.
- Ask them to sign a short document affirming their permission.

The following document provides an example of how these processes are presented to participants and documented. A consent form not only provides information, but is a record of consent, so that copies should be provided to each signatory.

YOUTH RECREATIONAL FACILITIES IN LEDDINGHALL

Mrs. Miles' ninth-grade class at Leddinghall High School is concerned that no recreational facilities for young people are available in the district. They are now engaged in reviewing the services, facilities, and resources available to young people in the community and will invite young people who live there to tell of their experiences. On the basis of this study, the class will write a report on recreation for young people in the Leddinghall community to be presented to the town council.

Consent Form

I, _____ have read the above information and been informed of the nature of the study. I consent to being interviewed by a class member for this study. I understand that:

- All information will be kept confidential
- I may withdraw from the study at any time and have information I have given returned to me at that time
- I will not be identified in any way in reports arising from this study without my written permission

Signed: _____

Date: _____

RESEARCH ETHICS

Ethical procedures are established by:

1. **Confidentiality:** Privacy is protected by ensuring confidentiality of information.
2. **Permissions:** Permission is obtained to carry out the research from people in positions of responsibility.
3. **Informed consent:** Participants are informed of the nature of the study and provide formal consent to be included.

VALIDITY IN ACTION RESEARCH: EVALUATING QUALITY

When teachers engage in research in their own classrooms, they are usually able to ascertain the worth of research according to its usefulness in helping them accomplish their teaching objectives. Studies wider in scope, however, involving official approval or requests for funding, often need to satisfy more stringent requirements. People want assurance that sloppy, poorly devised, or unbalanced research is not likely to result in inadequate or potentially damaging outcomes. In these circumstances they often require an examination of the rigor or strength of the procedures to be included in the research design sections of a proposal, or in the methodology section of a research report.

Action research, being essentially qualitative or naturalistic, seeks to construct holistic understandings of the dynamic and complex social world of classroom and school. It reveals people's subjective experience and the ways they meaningfully construct and interpret events, activities, behaviors, responses, and problems. Although these types of studies provide powerful understandings that enable the development of effective practices and activities, they are mostly specific to particular contexts and lack stability over time—what is true at one time may vary as policies and procedures shift and the actors in the setting change. When a new principal arrives at a school, or staff changes occur, for instance, then the life of the school is likely to change in significant ways. The truths emerging from naturalistic inquiry therefore are always contingent; that is, they are "true" only for the people, the time, and the setting of that particular study. We are not looking for "the truth" or "the causes," but "truths-in-context."

Procedures for evaluating the rigor of experimental or survey research evolve around well-formulated processes for testing reliability[5] and establishing the validity[6] of a study. Traditional experimental criteria for establishing validity, however, are inappropriate for

---

[5]Reliability is estimated by measures of the extent to which similar results may be expected from similar samples within the population studied, across different contexts and at different times. Reliability focuses on the stability of results across time, settings, and samples.

[6]Experimental validity is defined in two ways—external validity and internal validity. Measures of external validity estimate the probability that results obtained from the sample differ significantly from results we would expect. Internal validity focuses on the extent to which results obtained might be attributed to the dependent variables included in the study, and not some other cause. Researchers ask "Do our instruments actually measure what we wish them to measure?" and "Are the results attributal to the dependent variables we have stipulated, or to some other related variable?" Internal validity focuses on careful research design and instrumentation. Both reliability and validity are verified by statistical and other techniques.

qualitative action research, and debate continues about a broadly acceptable set of criteria to use for this purpose. Some researchers have approached this task by seeking to identify the foundational assumptions underlying the term *validity*. "What does it mean," they ask, "when we seek to establish the 'validity' of a study?" Two highly respected scholars, Denzin and Lincoln (1998b, p. 414), interpret validity to mean:

> . . . a text's call to authority and truth . . .is established through recourse to a set of rules concerning knowledge, its production, and representation. The rules, as Scheurich (1992, p. 1) notes, if properly followed, establish validity. Without validity there is not truth, and without truth there can be no trust in a text's claims to validity. . . . Validity becomes a boundary line that "divides good research from bad, separates acceptable (to a particular research community) research from unacceptable research . . ." (Scheurich, 1992, p. 5).

Because qualitative methods are essentially subjective in nature and local in scope, procedures for assessing the validity of research are quite different than those used for experimental study. As the previous quote suggests, a new set of criteria is required to provide people with trust that the research is acceptable. A common set of criteria for establishing the validity of research has been provided by Lincoln and Guba (1985). They suggest that because there can be no objective measures of validity, the underlying issue is to identify ways of establishing *trustworthiness*, the extent to which we can trust the truthfulness or adequacy of a research project. They propose that means for establishing trustworthiness involve procedures for attaining:

- **Credibility:** The plausibility and integrity of a study.
- **Transferability:** Whether results might be applied to other contexts than the research setting.
- **Dependability:** Research processes are clearly defined and open to scrutiny.
- **Confirmability:** The outcomes of the study are demonstrably drawn from the data.

Trustworthiness, therefore, is established by recording and reviewing the research procedures themselves to establish the extent to which they ensure that the phenomena studied are accurately and adequately represented. The following procedures are adapted from those suggested by Guba and Lincoln.

Credibility

Qualitative research is easily open to sloppy, biased processes that merely reinscribe the biases and perspectives of those in control of the research process. Careful adherence to the following processes assists researchers in minimizing the extent to which their own viewpoints intrude. They may also review and record the following features of the research process to provide evidence of rigorous procedure, which enhances the plausibility of their findings (Lincoln & Guba, 1985).

Prolonged Engagement Brief visits to a research site provide only superficial understandings of events. A rigorous study requires researchers to invest sufficient time to achieve a relatively sophisticated understanding of a context: to learn the intricacies of cultural knowledge and meaning that sustain people's actions and activities in a setting. Prolonged engagement in a setting also enables researchers to establish relationships of trust with participants, allowing them to gain greater access to "insider" knowledge rather than the often superficial or purposeful information given to strangers. Researchers therefore add to the credibility of a study by extending and recording the time spent in the research context.

Persistent Observation Being present in the research context for an extended time period is not a sufficient condition to establish credibility, however. Sometimes researchers mistake their presence in the field for engagement in research. In a recent study one investigator indicated he had worked with a group of teachers for months. He had, however, not engaged in systematic research at that time and his "observations" were undirected, unfocused, and unrecorded. Participants need to consciously engage in data collection activities to provide depth to their inquiries. This is essential to interviewing processes, as a single interview lasting 15 to 20 minutes provides very superficial understandings that lack both detail and adequacy. Prolonged engagement signals the need for repeated, extended interviews to establish the adequacy, accuracy, and appropriateness of research materials. Researchers therefore need to record the number and duration of observations and interviews.

Triangulation Triangulation involves the use of multiple and different sources, methods, and perspectives to corroborate, elaborate, or illuminate the research problem and its outcomes. It enables the inquirer to clarify meaning by identifying different ways the phenomenon is being perceived (Stake, 2005). In action research we include all stakeholders relevant to the issue investigated, observe multiple sites and events relevant to the stakeholders and issue investigated, and review all relevant materials, including resources, reports, records, research literature, and so on. These multiple sources and methods provide rich resources for building adequate and appropriate accounts and understandings that form the base for working toward the resolution of research problems.

Participant Debriefing This process is similar to *peer debriefing* as proposed by Lincoln and Guba (1985), but differs because of the change in the status of the researcher in an action research process. It is not solely the research facilitator who is in need of debriefing, but other participants in the process as well. Debriefing is a process of exposing oneself to a disinterested person for the purpose of exploring and challenging aspects of the inquiry that might otherwise remain implicit only within the participant's mind (Lincoln & Guba, 1985). The purposes of debriefing are to review the appropriateness of research procedures and to clarify the participant's ways of describing and interpreting events. Debriefing also provides participants with an opportunity for catharsis, enabling them to deal with emotions and feelings that might cloud their vision or prevent relevant information from emerging. Researcher facilitators often provide debriefing sessions with research participants, but may also require an interested colleague to engage in debriefing them on the processes of research they are guiding. The credibility of a study is enhanced when researchers record debriefing opportunities given to participants.

Diverse Case Analysis In all research it is necessary to ensure that other interpretations of the data are fully explored. Sometimes there is a temptation to include in a research process only those people who are positively inclined toward the issue under study, or to interpret the information in particular ways. Diverse case analysis seeks to ensure that all possible perspectives are taken into account, and that the interpretations of important, significant, or powerful people do not overwhelm others. Diverse case analysis enables participants to constantly refine interpretations so that all participant perspectives are included in the final report, and all issues are dealt with. The credibility of a study is enhanced if researchers can demonstrate that all perspectives affecting the study have been included. A clear statement of sampling procedures assists in this process.

Referential Adequacy Referential adequacy refers to the need for concepts and structures of meaning within the study to clearly reflect the perspectives, perceptions, and language of participants. When participants' experiences and perspectives are reinterpreted through the lenses of other existing reports or theories, or in terms derived from existing practices, procedures, or policies, research outcomes are likely to be distorted. One of the key features of qualitative research is the need to ensure that interpretations are "experience-near," grounded in the language and terminology used by participants to frame and describe their experience. Where it is necessary to use more general terms to refer to a number of phenomena, those terms should adequately apply to the specific details to which they refer. The credibility of a study is enhanced to the extent that researchers can demonstrate that outcomes of the study have a direct relationship to the terminology and language used by participants.

Member Checks In experimental inquiry, research subjects rarely have the opportunity to question or review the information gathered and the outcomes of the study. The practical nature of action research, however, requires that participants be given frequent opportunity to review the raw data, the analyzed data, and reports that are produced. This process of review is called *member checking* and provides the means for ensuring that the research adequately and accurately represents the perspectives and experiences of participants. Member checking is one of the key procedures required to establish the credibility of a study.

Transferability

Unlike quantitative research that assumes the need to generalize the results of the study, qualitative research by its very nature can only apply results directly to the context of the study. Nevertheless, researchers seek to provide the possibility that results might be transferred to other settings to enable people to take advantage of the knowledge acquired in the course of the study. Whether such application is possible, it is assumed, can be assessed according to the likelihood that another context is sufficiently similar to allow results to be applicable. A study from rural Australia, for instance, may or may not have importance for suburban Holland. Qualitative research reports seek to provide sufficiently detailed descriptions of the context and the participants to enable others to assess the likely applicability of the research to their own situation. Thickly detailed descriptions therefore contribute to the trustworthiness of a study by enabling other audiences to clearly understand the nature of the context and the people participating in the study.

Dependability

Trustworthiness also depends on the extent to which observers are able to ascertain whether research procedures are adequate for the purposes of the study. Where insufficient information is available, or available information indicates the likelihood of superficial and/or limited inquiry, observers will not feel the study is dependable. The dependability of research is achieved through an *inquiry audit* whereby details of the research process—including processes for defining the research problem, collecting and analyzing data, and constructing reports—are made available to participants and other audiences.

Confirmability

Confirmability is achieved through an audit trail, the inquirer having retained recorded information that can be made available for review. This information includes raw data such as field notes, photographs, diary entries, original and annotated documents, copies of letters and materials generated at meetings, and so on. Data reduction and analysis products are also included, as well as plans and reports derived from the study. This information enables participants or other observers to be able to confirm that research accurately and adequately represents the perspectives presented in the study. By this means they enhance the trustworthiness of the study.

Validity and Participation

The strength of qualitative research derives from the methodological intent to build accounts that more clearly represent the experience, perspective, and voice of those studied. The credibility of accounts, to some extent, is derived from the extent to which researchers are able to enact the procedures delineated in the previous section. Throughout the process, however, researchers constantly run the risk of observing and interpreting events through the lens of their own history of experience, thus putting the validity of the study at risk (Stringer & Genat, 1998).

A much greater degree of credibility, however, is gained through the use of participatory processes. When research participants engage in the processes of collecting and analyzing data, they are in a position to constantly check and extend the veracity of the material with which they are working. As they read the data of their interviews, they not only "see themselves" more clearly (the looking-glass-self), but are drawn to extend and clarify the events they describe. As they engage in data analysis, they are able to identify more clearly and correctly the significant experiences and features as well as the elements of which they are comprised. As they assist in the construction of reports they help formulate accounts that more clearly use familiar language to represent their experience and perspective.

Participatory processes respond to recent developments in qualitative research (Altheide & Johnson, 1998) that point to the multiple means now used to establish validity, according to the nature and purposes of the study and the theoretical frames of reference upon which the research rests. In a very direct way, engaging people as direct participants in the research also enables a study to take into account such issues as emotionality, caring, subjective understanding, and relationships in research (Haraway, 1988; Lather, 1993; Oleson, 1998, 2005), which are important features of feminist research. They are incorporated as a means of ensuring the validity/trustworthiness of a study, but also enhance the possibility of effective change.

Validity and Utility

One of the greatest sources of validity in action research is the utility of the outcomes of research. Where participants are able to construct ways of describing and interpreting events that enable them to take effective action on the issue they have investigated, they demonstrate the validity of the research. The power of the processes is nowhere more evident than in effective actions emerging from the research, clearly demonstrating the success in identifying appropriate perspectives and meanings. High degrees of credibility are evident, since the understandings that emerge from the processes of inquiry are successfully applied to actions within the research setting. It becomes immediately evident that the features on which the research has focused are adequate to account for the phenomena investigated.

SUMMARY

Establishing Validity

The validity of action research is verified through procedures establishing credibility, transferability, dependability, confirmability, degrees of participation, and utility. These are attained through:

1. *Prolonged engagement:* The duration of the research processes.
2. *Persistent observation:* The number and duration of observations and interviews.
3. *Triangulation:* All sources of data, including the settings observed, the stakeholders interviewed, and materials reviewed.
4. *Participant debriefing:* Processes for reviewing research procedures.
5. *Negative case analysis:* Processes for ensuring that a diversity of interpretations is explored.
6. *Referential adequacy:* How terminology within the study is drawn from participant language and concepts.
7. *Member checks:* Procedures for checking the accuracy of data, and the appropriateness of data analysis and reporting.
8. *Transferability:* The inclusion of detailed descriptions of the participants and the research context.
9. *Dependability:* Detailed description of the research process.
10. *Confirmability:* The data available for review.
11. *Participation:* The extent of stakeholder participation in the research process.
12. *Utility:* Practical outcomes of the research process.

Gathering Data:
Sources of
Information

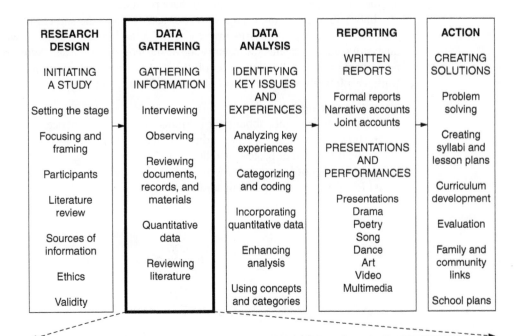

RESEARCH DESIGN	DATA GATHERING	DATA ANALYSIS	REPORTING	ACTION
INITIATING A STUDY	GATHERING INFORMATION	IDENTIFYING KEY ISSUES AND EXPERIENCES	WRITTEN REPORTS	CREATING SOLUTIONS
Setting the stage	Interviewing	Analyzing key experiences	Formal reports Narrative accounts Joint accounts	Problem solving
Focusing and framing	Observing		PRESENTATIONS AND PERFORMANCES	Creating syllabi and lesson plans
Participants	Reviewing documents, records, and materials	Categorizing and coding		Curriculum development
Literature review		Incorporating quantitative data	Presentations Drama Poetry	Evaluation
Sources of information	Quantitative data	Enhancing analysis	Song Dance Art	Family and community links
Ethics	Reviewing literature		Video Multimedia	
Validity		Using concepts and categories		School plans

Contents of the Chapter

First phase of inquiry is in which participants focus their investigation and design a valid and ethical research process. This chapter presents the first steps of that investigation, describing procedures for systematically accumulating information that will contribute to extended understandings of the issue investigated. It provides details of:

- the *purposes* for gathering information.
- procedures for *interviewing* participants.
- procedures for *observing* settings and events.
- procedures for reviewing *artifacts*—records, documents, and materials.
- procedures for incorporating *quantitative data*, including those obtained from *surveys*.
- procedures for reviewing the *literature*.

From Chapter 4 of *Action Research in Education*, Second Edition. Ernie Stringer. Copyright © 2008 by Pearson Education, Inc. All rights reserved.

BUILDING A PICTURE: GATHERING INFORMATION

A basic research routine is to *look*: gathering information; *think*: analyzing the information; *act*: taking action on the basis of that analysis (see Figure 1). The routine was used to clarify the issue being investigated, to build a preliminary picture of the people and the context, and to design a research plan.

This chapter focuses on the first phase of that research plan—gathering information relevant to the research question that emerged as part of the research plan. It is, in effect, the "look" phase of research, in which research participants gather information from a variety of sources that might shed light on the issue investigated. They are, in effect, extending the picture that emerged from preliminary planning activities.

Information can come from a variety of sources, and the sources used will be determined by the nature of the issue investigated. If a teacher is not satisfied with the level or quality of student learning, for instance, he or she would need to ask "Why are my students not learning at a level I might expect of them?" To answer this question he or she needs to consider information from a variety of sources. The teacher might:

- **Observe** students at work.
- Have students **talk** about their learning/classroom experience.
- **Talk** with colleagues, school administrators, and/or parents.
- **Read** research or professional literature.
- Review **records and documentation** of past student performance.
- Identify available **materials and resources.**

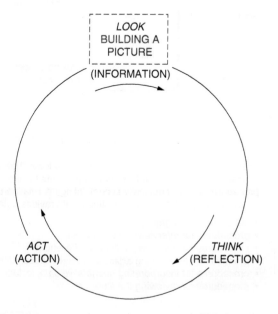

Figure 1
Look: Gathering Information

The teacher would select from these sources according to the level of difficulty he or she is experiencing. Simpler, routine planning processes may require minimal inputs from only some of these sources. More complex or longstanding problems that fail to respond to routine teaching processes may require more extended exploration and may include any or all of the resources just listed.

The following sections therefore provide guidance for systematically acquiring relevant information. They include procedures for:

- Interviewing
- Focus groups
- Participant observation
- Reviewing artifacts—documents, records, materials, and equipment
- Conducting a survey
- Gathering numerical and statistical information
- Reviewing literature

Each of these types of information has the potential to increase the power and scope of the research process. If we not only listen to people describe and interpret their experience, but observe and participate in events, and read reports of those or similar events, then we enrich the research process. The use of multiple sources diminishes the possibility that one perspective alone will shape the course or determine the outcomes of investigation, and provides a diversity of materials from which to fashion effective solutions to the problem. This **triangulation** of data adds depth and rigor to the research process.

INTERVIEWING: GUIDED CONVERSATIONS

One of the major purposes of this phase of inquiry is to understand how students are experiencing classroom and school events and activities. When we work with children who are disengaged, disinterested, or misbehaving, for instance, we ask "What is happening for this child? What aspect of the child's experience is creating these responses to the situation?" This approach differs from the detached, clinical perspective of the psychologist, another useful viewpoint, who may explain those behaviors in terms of behavioral or personality disorders—depression, anxiety, attention deficit disorder, and so on. In action research, however, we seek to understand the natural world of the child, and to understand it in the child's terms.

I've heard many stories of children refusing to go to school or misbehaving badly and subsequent investigations revealing reasons for their behavior—a child who feared the departure of her mother after a parental argument; another scared to go school because he didn't have the right pens; one who was scared of a bully; another whose brother had been sent to prison. In many cases this became apparent only when the child was asked to talk at length about his or her experience and provided the basis for effective actions to deal with the issue. Children are like adults in many ways. We can't assume that we all understand ourselves perfectly, but what knowledge and understanding we have needs to be taken seriously when actions are taken that affect our lives.

The same is true for other research participants—colleagues, parents, administrators, and so on. Interviews enable them to describe the situation from their own perspective and to interpret events in their own terms. They enable other participants to "enter the world" of the person interviewed and to understand events from their perspective (Denzin, 1997; Spradley, 1979a, Spradley & McCurdy, 1972). Interviews not only provide a record of their views and perspectives, but also symbolically recognize the legitimacy of their points of view. The interview process, however, also provides opportunities for participants to revisit and reflect on events in their lives, and in the process, to extend their understanding of their own experience. This double hermeneutic—or meaning-making process—serves as the principal powerhouse of the research process, enabling all participants to extend their understanding of their own and other's experience. In classroom terms, the teacher has a greater understanding of the experience and perspective of the student, and vice versa.

Interviewing is best accomplished as a sociable series of events, not unlike a conversation between friends, where the easy exchange of information takes place in a comfortable, friendly environment. Although some people envisage interviewing as a form of authentic dialogue, we need to be wary of the way this "dialogue" emerges. When interviewers engage in exchanges of information or experience, as in a normal conversation, they unwittingly inscribe their own sets of meanings into the research process, constructing descriptions and interpretations that easily distort the experience or perspective of the participant interviewed. Authentic dialogue can only occur when a research facilitator is a natural participant in the setting, and when other participants have had opportunities to explore their own experience prior to engaging in dialogue. The following protocols provide ways to engage the interview process comfortably, ethically, and productively.

A wide range of literature provides information about interviewing (e.g., Chirban, 1996; Holstein & Gubrium, 1995; Kvale, 1996; McCracken, 1988; Rubin & Rubin 1995). Researchers should use these materials selectively, however, since some interview techniques are used for clinical or hypothesis-testing processes not suited to the purposes of action research. The key issue guiding the selection of a technique is whether it is used to reveal the perspective of the participant or whether it focuses on revealing specified types of information.

Although interviewing can be very time consuming, the processes are very productive, enabling research participants to explore an issue in some depth and, in the process, to develop understanding, trust, and good working relationships. In teaching terms, interviews provide the means to accomplish a wide range of student learning outcomes. Where time does not permit widespread use of interviews, focus groups provide a similar means for accomplishing the data gathering potential of interviews. By using group activities in the classroom teachers can provide stimulating and informative exploration of issues that enables students to enter an action research process (see following discussion).

Initiating Interviews: Establishing Relationships of Trust

Initial stages of the interview process can be a little uncomfortable for both interviewer and interviewee, and the interviewer must establish a relationship of trust in order to enable interviewees to feel comfortable in revealing their experiences, either to a stranger or a colleague. Initial contacts with people to inform them of the issue being studied and explore the possibility of their participation is suggested. The researcher:

- identifies him- or herself.
- identifies the issue of interest.
- asks permission to talk about that issue.
- negotiates a convenient time and place to meet.

The actual conversation might sound something like the following:

"Hi! I'm Ernie Stringer. The principal says he's informed staff I'd be working here. I've been asked to assist staff to explore ways of improving parent–teacher conferences. I'd like to hear your views about that. Could we set up a time to talk? I'd need about half an hour of your time."

The prime directive in interviewing is for the interviewee to feel comfortable and safe when talking with the interviewer. The pertinent information should be presented in ways appropriate to the people and the setting, and that enable people to feel in control of the situation—to make them feel they're not being "put upon." Provide them with opportunities to determine the time and place of interviews, and ask them to suggest places to meet where they are comfortable. A classroom or school office may not be the best place to interview children or parents—the site itself might put them into a particular role or frame of mind. Behavior and talk are greatly influenced by the environment in which they occur. Research is a sociable process and should be treated as such. According to the circumstances, people may be comfortable in their own homes, in cafes or fast food outlets, or in a park or other public place. A meeting over coffee enables interviewer and interviewee to chat about general events and establish a conversational tone in their interactions. This provides a context to move easily to the issue of interest.

Initiating interviews is sometimes a sensitive issue. You might manage, initially, short chats in hallways and lounges, which open possibilities for more extended "conversations" (interviews). It's important to keep these initial occasions low key and informal, so people feel they aren't being imposed upon. After an initial interaction, you might indicate your desire to have them speak at greater length about issues arising in your conversation. Let them know of the focus of your interests and that you're interested in their perspective. "This has been interesting, Jack. I'd like to be able to explore this issue further. Could we meet somewhere and continue this conversation?" This provides a context for commencing more in-depth "conversations" that provide the basis for a continuing research relationship.

Questioning Techniques

Spradley (1979a) provides a useful framework of questions derived from his attempts to elicit natural structures of meaning used by people to describe and organize their social worlds. His essentially ethnographic methodology seeks neutral, nonleading questions that minimize the extent to which participant responses will be governed by frameworks of meaning inadvertently imposed by the researcher. A modified form of this framework provides the means to engage research participants in extended interviews revealing detailed descriptions of events and interactions in their lives and providing opportunities to explore significant issues in depth on their own terms.

A major problem with the interview process is that researcher perceptions, perspectives, interests, and agendas easily flavor questions, but the central purpose of the process is to obtain *interviewee* perspectives. Common approaches to interviewing based on extended lists of predefined questions are therefore inappropriate for the purpose of this type of research. Ethnographic interviews are quite different from questionnaires that frame the issue in terms making sense to the researcher, often focusing on technical/professional concepts, agendas, procedures, or practices. This detracts from the ability of participants to define, describe, and interpret experiences in their own terms, and can sometimes alienate audiences central to the study. Questionnaires, therefore, usually are inappropriate in the early stages of action research. At later stages of the process they may be used to gather data from a broader audience but care must be taken to frame them in terms derived from participants' concepts and terminology (see discussion later in the chapter).

First Phase: Grand Tour Questions An action research interview begins with one general "grand tour" question taking the form:

"Tell me about . . ." For example, "Tell me about your work." "Tell me about your school."

Though there are many extensions from this fundamental query, the simple framing enables respondents to describe, frame, and interpret events, issues, and other phenomena in their own terms. The question is not asked in bald isolation, but emerges contextually when sufficient rapport between participants has been established. It is also necessary to *frame* or contextualize the question:

"There are a number of people in this school concerned about [students dropping out of school]. Last time we talked you spoke briefly about this issue. Could you *tell me about* [students dropping out of your school]?"

Often it is best to contextualize the issue by starting with a more general question:

"Last time we spoke of [students dropping out of your school]. I'm not very familiar with your school. Could you *tell me about* your school?"

In most cases people are able to talk at length on an issue about which they are concerned. It merely requires a listener with an attentive attitude to enable them to engage in an extended discourse, sometimes encouraged by prompts (described next) to extend their descriptions. In some instances, however, participants may be unable to answer such a general question, tempting the researcher to insert more specific questions that destroy the intent of the research process. Spradley (1979a) suggests alternative ways of asking grand tour questions when respondents are able only to give limited responses to the more general question:

- **Typical** grand tour questions, enabling respondents to talk of ways events usually occur (e.g., How does your group usually work? Describe a typical day in your school.).
- **Specific** grand tour questions, which focus on particular events or times (e.g., Can you tell me about yesterday's meeting? Describe what happened the last time.).
- **A guided tour** question is a request for an actual tour that allows participants to show researchers (and, where possible, other stakeholders) around their offices, schools, classrooms, centers, or agencies (e.g., Could you show me around your

classroom/school?). As they walk around the school or classroom, participants may explain details about the people and activities involved in each part of the setting.

- **A task-related** grand tour question aids in description (e.g., Could you draw me a map of the school/classroom?). Maps are often very instructive and provide opportunities for extensive description and questioning. You can also ask participants to demonstrate how things are done (e.g., Can you show me how you write up your syllabus? Can you show me how the children do this work?).

Grand tour questions comprise ways of initiating participant descriptions of their experience. Information acquired in this way provides the basis for more extended descriptions, elicited by similar types of questions but emerging from ideas and agendas within the respondent's own descriptions.

Novice researchers sometimes find interviewing an uncomfortable experience—working through structured questioning processes seems awkward and unnatural. It seems impossible that such a discomfiting process would enable people to speak freely, and they tend to fall back on "conversation" as a means of engaging participants. Practice and experience, however, show how it is possible for interview questions to freely and easily construct a conversation. In their best formulation, questions should emerge in a fashion similar to the streetwise informality inherent in media presentations of urban youth: "What's happenin', man? What's goin' down? What's up?"

Novice researchers should prepare for interviewing processes by memorizing the forms of questioning described next and practicing mock interviews with friends and colleagues until they are able to translate the rather formal interview structures suggested in this text into the common language of the contexts they engage. Like any set of skills, practice may not make perfect, but it certainly increases effectiveness.

An interesting outcome of the acquisition of these questioning skills is their application to educational contexts. Teachers will find them wonderful tools for classroom questioning procedures, and administrators will find them useful in defining their managerial work—consultation, planning, leadership, and organization. A teacher wrote of this work in a message to a colleague:

> Spradley's format is very helpful when I apply it for interviewing my kids. I use the visual cues, have them write stuff out on paper, make drawings, maps of the school. The work is shared. We physically walk the area—a guided tour. I first thought the idea was dumb, but it's a great success. It's engaged, it's shared, we are walking together. The movement stops the tape in the head. The experience is shared. It's generative.

Second Phase: Extending the Interview—Mini-Tour Questions Interviews emerge and expand from responses to the initial grand tour questions. As people respond to the initial grand tour questions, a number of details begin to emerge, revealing events, activities, issues, and so on that comprise their experience and perspective. Sometimes the information is limited and interviewers need to probe further to enable the respondent to "dig deeper" into his or her experience. At this stage, the source of further questions emerges

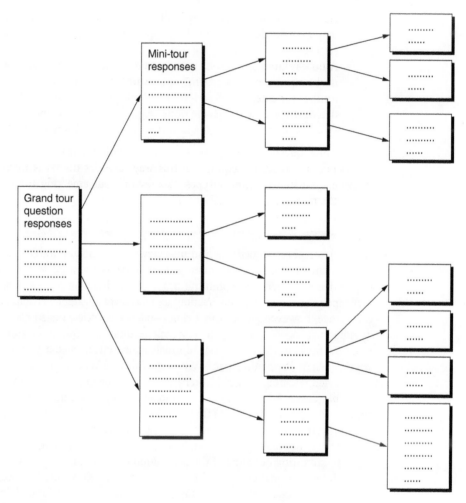

Figure 2
Mini-Tour Questioning Processes

from concepts, issues, and ideas embedded in respondent answers to the first questions. The interviewer asks *mini-tour* questions that enable interviewees to extend their responses (see Figure 2).

Mini-tour questions are similar in form to the general, typical, specific, guided, and task-related grand tour questions, but the focus of the questions is derived from information revealed in initial responses. They take forms such as the following:

"You talked of the way students start their work in the morning. *Tell me more about* students starting their work."
"Tell me how your students *usually* start their work."
"Tell me how your students started their work *this morning.*"

"Can we *sit in your room* and have you tell me what's happening as students start their work?"

"Can you *show me* how students start their work?"

Responses to these questions may lead to other mini-tour questions that eventually provide extended, detailed descriptions of the issues and contexts investigated.

Extending Participant Responses: Prompt Questions Further information may be acquired through the skillful use of "prompts," which enable participants to reveal more details of the phenomena they are discussing. For example:

- **Extension** questions (e.g., "Tell me more about . . .," "Is there anything else you can tell me about . . .," "What else can you tell me about . . .?"
- **Encouragement** comments/questions (e.g., "Go on." "Yes?" "Uh-huh?")
- **Example** questions (e.g., "Can you give me an example of how children start their work?")

Prompt questions are not designed to elicit particular types of information the interviewer might see as desirable, but merely to enable the interviewee to think more closely about the events or perspectives described.

As interviews progress, research facilitators may be presented with viewpoints that appear limited, biased, wrong, or potentially harmful. They should not, however, attempt to extend the participant's responses by suggesting appropriate responses—such as "Don't you think that . . ."—and definitely must avoid discussion or debate about information presented. They should certainly avoid criticizing the perspective presented or suggesting alternative acceptable viewpoints. Acceptance of diverse viewpoints is a prime directive in action research, even where those perspectives conflict dramatically with those of other research participants. Challenges to particular viewpoints will occur naturally as differing perspectives are presented in more public arenas. The task at this stage, to employ the words of a well-known anthropologist, is "to grasp the natives' point of view, to realize their vision of their world" (Malinowski, 1922/1961, p. 5).

In the course of work with senior government department managers, my Aboriginal colleagues and I sometimes faced people whose perspectives were fundamentally racist. I would converse with them with barely controlled rage, fuming at the insensitive nature of their remarks. On one occasion an Aboriginal colleague later said "Take it easy, Stringer. He doesn't understand," to which I responded, "How do you stand it?" He looked at me quizzically and said, "You just get used to it." In many of these situations we were able to engage in productive work with these departments that, in the longer term, sensitized the people with whom we had been speaking to their inappropriate behavior and/or perspectives. I learned at that time that immediate confrontation is not always an appropriate response to inappropriate speech or behavior.

Prolonged Engagement The intent of action research is to assist people to develop new understandings of issues or problems. Asking them to "explain" superficially why and how the issue affects them often tends merely to elicit taken-for-granted responses or perspectives that reproduce existing understandings and provide little basis for revealing underlying features of their experience. Interview processes should give people the opportunity to carefully explore their experience, examining how events and issues are embedded in the complex features of their everyday lives.

The questioning techniques previously described help facilitate this descriptive process, but can usually only be effective if sufficient time is allocated to enable participants to explore the issue in depth. While simple problems or issues may require relatively small investments of time, larger or long-standing issues require prolonged periods of reflection and analysis. While a single 15- to 20-minute interview may suffice for a simple issue, significant issues require more than a superficial exploration. Multiple interviews of 30 to 60 minutes' duration enable participants to explore issues in depth, engaging the multiple dimensions of their experience and, in the process, extending their understanding of the complexity of the issues they face.

Except for in simple research processes, repeat interviews are therefore an essential feature of good qualitative research. Repeat interviews not only enable participants to reflect on issues more extensively, but provide opportunities to review and extend information previously acquired. Extended engagement therefore suggests the need for a significant time commitment, and repeated interaction with or between research participants. Merely being in the context is not sufficient—one must be engaged in systematic inquiry required to *re-search* an issue within a context.

When I queried the extent of the engagement of one researcher, she replied, "Oh, I was working with these teachers for months." Unfortunately, the intensive nature of the project work in which teachers and researchers were engaged provided little opportunity for them to discuss the nature of their experience, most of their attention being focused on the technical issues related to the project. The single 15-minute interview for each teacher was an inadequate vehicle for revealing the complex nature of their experience, providing only superficial comments that were uninformative and uninspiring.

Recording Information

Although action research processes often are informal, especially in small-scale or localized projects, it is important to keep a record of information acquired. This is especially important when different groups are involved, when personality differences are likely to create discord, or when sensitive issues are investigated. Participants acquire a degree of safety in knowing their perspectives are not forgotten or distorted over time. For reasons of accuracy and harmony, an ongoing record of information is a central feature of research. Field notes and tape recordings provide the two major forms of recording, of information, though increasing use is being made of video recording.

Field Notes
Verbatim Record Wherever possible, interviewees should make an immediate record of responses. You should ask permission for this before the interview, or in some cases, after the first few minutes, when the person has commenced talking. "This is very interesting. Do

On numerous occasions I have been engaged in action research projects that threatened to be disrupted by disputes about things people had said or decisions that had been made. Referring back to the recorded data and reading the actual words people had used usually restores order when disputes threaten to erupt. In numerous instances a molli-fied participant has acknowledged his or her error by saying "Did I say that?" or "I for-got that we'd decided that."

you mind if I take notes as you talk?" Handwritten field notes are a common form of record-ing, wherein researchers write a verbatim record of people's actual words. This requires researchers to be constantly aware of the need to record what is actually *said* by the person being interviewed, rather than a condensed or "tidied up" version. It is a "warts and all" procedure, where colloquialisms, incorrect grammar, or even blatantly incorrect informa-tion are precisely recorded. This all goes into the mix to ensure an accurate and authentic account of the person's perspective. At later stages of the interview (see the following "Member Checking" discussion) the interviewee will have opportunities to correct or add to the information given.

The following example is a record of an interview with a middle school teacher:

Interviewer: Some teachers say they'd like greater parent participation in this school. Can you tell me what you think of the idea of greater parent participation?

Teacher: Well, parents should feel they are part of the school. . . . We could provide, like, inservices for parents on things like handling children, using computers . . . you know, inspiration, web searches.

It would help parents to have skills to assist their kids, especially those who are struggling. Parents could be offered stuff at low cost, no cost—like study skills, how to develop study habits with children. It'd be low pressure, low key. You could have staff volunteers with special skills, special expertise.

It helps establish good relationships with parents. Give them greater ability to communicate results. They'd be able to talk more easily about their children.

Interviewer: Are there other ways to increase parent participation?

Teacher: I like having parents in class who can guide and help a child, but not do the work for the kids. Some parents help, but they end up doing the work for the kids. That's not on. But if they help the kids with their work, it's a great help to me.

One school had a parent scheduled to help a child. They'd have that child each time they came to the classroom, helping with, like, reading, if the child was having difficulty with reading. . . .

This type of handwritten record requires practice in writing at speed and the con-comitant development of personal "shorthand" writing protocols—"&" for "and," "w/" for "with," "t" for "the," "g" for "-ing," missing consonants (e.g., *writg*, or *wrtg* for *writing*), and so on. It takes practice, but is essential if researchers are to record the respondent's actual words. Those responsible for recording information need to be wary of paraphrasing or abstracting, since this defeats the purpose of interviewing, which is to capture the voice of participants, describing things as they would describe them. Sometimes it may be necessary to ask the person interviewed to repeat information, or to pause momentarily so the interviewee can "catch up" on note taking.

Member Checking Once an interview has finished, the interviewer should read back the notes, giving the respondent an opportunity to confirm the accuracy of the notes, or to extend or clarify information given. In some cases it may also be possible to identify the key features of the interview to use in data analysis. Some people type their notes and have the respondent read them to check for accuracy. It may also be appropriate, in some instances, to provide a copy of the field notes to the respondent for his or her own information.

Tape Recorders Using a tape recorder has the advantage of allowing the researcher to acquire a detailed and accurate account of an interview. Researchers acquire large quantities of information from multiple sources, so they should keep a careful record of their tapes, noting on each tape the person, place, time, and date of the interview. Tapes should be transcribed as soon as possible after the interview, and the accuracy of the resulting text should be verified by the person interviewed.

Tape recordings have a number of disadvantages, however, and researchers should carefully weigh the merits of this technology. Technical difficulties with equipment may damage rapport with respondents, and people sometimes find it difficult to talk freely in the presence of a recording device, especially when sensitive issues are discussed. A researcher may need to wait until a reasonable degree of rapport has been established before introducing the possibility of using a tape recorder. When using a recorder, the researcher should be prepared to stop the tape to allow respondents to speak "off the record" if they show signs of discomfort.

The sheer volume of material obtained through tape recording also may inhibit the steady progress of a research process. If tape recordings are used, they should be transcribed immediately so the relevant information becomes available to participants. This is particularly useful when contentious or sensitive issues are explored, since a person's own words may help resolve potentially inflammatory situations. Researchers should be wary of accumulating tapes for later transcribing—transcription is a lengthy and tedious process that may detract from the power of the research.

Interviewing Children

Action research works on the premise that children are active constructors of their own knowledge. By talking, listening, and reflecting on events within a system of mutually supportive relations, children are able to extend their understanding of events and experiences. An extensive literature has revealed the possibilities of engaging children in research processes related to their own learning environments.

Some researchers, however, initially find interviews with children to be somewhat problematic. Young children, especially, sometimes have difficulty engaging in the forms of discourse common to adults, and tend to respond or react to events in immediate rather than abstract terms. Asking children a grand tour question such as "Tell me about . . ." sometimes elicits an abbreviated or noncommittal response—"What do you want to know?" "I just like it!"—or a quizzical look.

In these circumstances, alternate forms of grand tour questions, especially those involving activity, may enhance opportunities to elicit responses from children and enable them to explore and express their experiences. These include:

Typical grand tour questions—"What usually happens. . . .?"
Specific grand tour questions—"What happened last time the class . . .?
Guided tour questions—"Can you show me around your classroom and tell me . . .?
Task-related questions—"Can you show me how . . .?" "Draw me a picture of . . ."

This latter form provides multiple ways for children to express their thoughts and feelings, or to reveal details of their experience. Activity questions are particularly fruitful in work with children. Art enables children to draw and talk about aspects of their experience. Care needs to taken to ensure the child is engaging actual events, rather than extrapolating to an imaginary world, as creative children sometimes do. You might ask the child to draw some aspects of his or her experience by requesting "Can you draw me a picture of . . .?" Then "Tell me about the picture."

In some cases, especially where sensitive issues are explored, some people use scenarios, asking children to recount a story using imaginary or fictional characters representing types of actors in the context. Drawings or doll figures also may be used for these purposes. It also may be useful to use reversal questions such as, "If you were a teacher, what would you do if . . .?" or future-oriented questions such as, "What would happen if . . .?" The problem with these types of question, however, is the risk that children will engage in fantasies having little bearing on the reality at hand.

It is often difficult for children to talk openly and honestly with an adult, especially an authority figure such as a teacher. For this reason it is necessary to spend time and effort developing an easy and friendly relationship that allows a child to respond more empathetically to researchers. Teachers engaging in research in their class or school may need to develop a different type of relationship to enable children to speak freely. They may also provide training and practice in interviewing techniques so the children can interview each other. This is especially useful with older children, providing a safe environment for them to explore their experience. In these circumstances, group techniques (see "Using Focus Groups to Gather Data" section) that mask the identity of the participants can also be fruitful.

The time, place, and style of interviews with children are particularly important. Children are likely to feel uncomfortable if a teacher interviews them individually in a classroom. They may feel as if they are "in trouble," or wary of being asked to divulge information about their classmates. This is especially true of "problem" students who may be central to a research process. Where they are included as participants in the research process, however, the rewards are often enormous, providing children with increased ownership and understanding of events and activities occurring in their school or classroom.

As qualitative and naturalistic studies increasingly engage children, a variety of resources in the literature can assist researchers in including children in the processes of investigation (e.g., Edwards, Gandini, & Forman, 1993; Fine & Sandstrom, 1988; Graue & Walsh, 1998; Greig & Taylor, 1998; Helm, 1999; Malaguzzi, 1995; Meerdink, 1999; Selekman, 1997). It is essential that children are able to describe and interpret experiences in their own terms, rather than being asked to respond to questions derived from a teacher's or an adult's perceptions of what *should be* important for a child. Often there is a tendency

Rhonda Petty (1997) describes her methods of working with a small group of boys from her class. She met with them in their homes, at McDonald's, in parks, and on small excursions. She was amazed at the difference in their demeanor and communicativeness in these contexts. They talked animatedly and easily, a far cry from the rather silent and uneasy conversations possible in the school context. She was able to elicit a broad range of information and gain a much clearer understanding of the boys with whom she worked, and to provide a richly evocative account of the way those interactions dramatically changed the images she had formed of them.

for educational researchers to mentally list issues derived from their professional repertoire of experience—materials, lessons, learning processes, timetables, homework, reading, behavior, and so on. These issues may be of peripheral relevance to children as they focus on a more existential response to their situation. Ultimately we wish to understand children's experience and perceptions of the issue we are investigating. The process enables the children to clarify and extend their understanding of events and to be able to participate in plans to remedy the situation.

I have many times had my faith in the integrity and good sense of children confirmed in research activities. I have seen high school dropouts engaged in extended research processes culminating in the development of a new alternative high school in my city. I have seen how seriously even young elementary children engage processes of inquiry focusing on issues about which they are concerned. Children, even those labeled as "at risk" or "problems," generally respond intelligently and with passion when they are engaged as competent, intelligent persons, actively engaged as members of a team, rather than being treated as as "miscreants" or "students" subject to the often directive dictates of authority figures. The principles of participatory action research are especially rich and rewarding when applied to young people.

Using Focus Groups to Gather Data

Traditional research practices focus largely on gathering data from individuals and using that information for an abstracting process of analysis. Data gathering in action research, however, becomes more effective when individuals are able to explore their experiences interactively. Although it is important for people to have opportunities to explore issues individually in the early stages of inquiry, joint processes of collaborative inquiry considerably enhance the power of a research process. Individual interviews followed by focus group exploration provide a context for participants to share information and extend their understanding of issues.

In recent years focus groups have emerged as a useful way to engage people in processes of investigation, enabling people to share information and to "trigger" new ideas or insights. A focus group may be envisioned as a group interview, with questions providing a stimulus for capturing people's experiences and perspectives. It provides the means for including relatively large numbers of people in a research process, an important consideration in larger projects.

When we bring diverse groups of people or children together, however, we need to carefully manage the dynamics of interaction and discussion to ensure the productive operation of focus groups. Too easily they sometimes degenerate into "gab-fests" or "slinging matches" where unfocused discussions or argumentative interchanges damage the harmonious qualities characteristic of good action research. Literature providing guidance for focus group facilitation includes publications by Barbour and Kitzinger (1998), Morgan (1997a, 1997b), Morgan and Krueger (1997), Krueger (1994, 1997a, 1997b), Krueger and Casey (2000), and Greenbaum (2000).

Bringing People Together To initiate focus group explorations, the research facilitator should seek out opportunities to bring people together to discuss issues of common interest. "I've spoken with a number of people about this issue and some of them have similar views to yourself. Would you be willing to meet with them to talk about the issues you've raised?" Or, "As you know, I've been speaking with other teachers and many are concerned about. . . . Would you attend a meeting with people like Janet Jones, Bill Rochon, and Maria Garcia to discuss this issue?"

As with interviews, the time and the place must be conducive to the process. People should have adequate time to explore the issue, and should be in a place where they are comfortable and feel they can express their views and experiences freely. A rushed meeting during recess time, or in a common room where others can overhear, is likely to limit the information shared or to limit the types of interaction leading to positive working relationships between people. These issues are especially important when working with families or children. As with interviews, meetings away from school or other formal settings may be more conducive to the easy and communicative atmosphere that provides the basis for ongoing development of productive action research processes.

Initially, research facilitators may arrange focus group meetings for small groups of stakeholders, but as the processes of inquiry develop it may be fruitful to bring larger groups of participants together. Larger meetings become more productive when all individuals have opportunities to express their thoughts and experiences, so focus groups may be used to enable greater active participation of all people present. Information gathering is often concomitant with information processing (analysis or interpretation).

The size of groups is important, with four to six people being the optimal number in each group to enable everyone to participate effectively. When dealing with large groups, then, it is usually best to form subgroups, with each subgroup recording its exploration and reporting back to the whole group.

Focus Group Processes Research facilitators should ensure that focus group sessions are carefully planned and facilitated to ensure the productive use of time. It is all too easy for poorly prepared groups to degenerate into gossip sessions, to be dominated by a forceful person, or to create antagonisms derived from intemperate debates. As with data gathering, researchers may engage single focus groups, though multiple groups may be used

Focus groups can be used in many contexts, large and small. When I worked with staff of the Brazos School to facilitate an internal evaluation, I interviewed each person individually, then wrote a short joint report revealing issues emerging from these interactions. After staff had read the report I facilitated a focus group meeting, enabling them to clarify issues emerging in the report and to identify and prioritize issues on which they wished to take action. Because it was a small school, we were able to complete this process in only a few days.

On another occasion I worked with a small team of researchers to facilitate review of a large regional organization. We spoke with staff and clients at local centers, assisting them to talk of their perceptions of the purpose of the organization, the services it was providing, and the problems they perceived. We then facilitated focus group meetings of staff and clients in each locality, enabling them to clarify the issues that had emerged. Finally, representatives from each of these localities met to explore issues emerging from these meetings and to formulate an action plan. As a result of these activities the organization was restructured, resulting in more effective services and greatly increased activity. The process took six months, but was highly effective in revitalizing an organization that was in danger of closing.

productively when meeting with diverse groups of stakeholders. The following steps provide a basic procedure for running focus groups:

1. Set ground rules.
   - Each person should have opportunities to express their perspective.
   - All perspectives should be accepted nonjudgmentally.
2. Provide clear guidance.
   - Provide and display focus questions.
   - Designate a time frame for each section/question.
3. Designate a facilitator for each group to:
   - ensure each person has an equal chance to talk.
   - keep discussions on track.
   - monitor time.
4. Record group talk in each group.
   - Designate a person to record proceedings.
   - Record the details of each person's contribution, using their own words.
   - Where appropriate, each group should summarize their discussions, identifying and recording key features of experience and significant issues or problems.
5. Elicit feedback and clarification.
   - Bring groups together, ensuring adequate time is available for feedback and discussion.
   - Have each group present the summary of their discussions.
   - Provide opportunities for individuals within each group to extend or clarify points presented.

- The facilitator should ask questions of each group designed to have them clarify and extend their contributions.
- Ensure that new information emerging from this process is recorded.

6. Analyze combined information.
    - Identify common features across groups.
    - Identify divergent issues or perspectives.
    - Rank issues in order of priority.

7. What next: Plan for action.
    - Define what is to happen next: What actions are to be taken, who will be responsible for them, where and when they will be done, what resources are required, and who will organize these actions.
    - Designate a person to monitor these actions.
    - Designate a time and place to meet again to review progress.

The rather bland description of these procedures masks the exciting and rewarding possibilities emerging from dialogue, discussion, and personal interactions common in these types of processes. There are many benefits gained through these processes. By providing participants with the space and time to engage in open dialogue on issues about which they are deeply concerned, they gain increased clarity and understanding of those issues and begin to develop the productive personal relationships so important to the effective enactment of action research.

Focus Questions Focus groups require careful facilitation to ensure people are able to accomplish productive purposes in the time they spend together. The purpose for meeting should be clearly described by the facilitator, and discussion should be focused on specific issues related to that purpose. As with individual interviews, the major purpose of these types of sessions is to provide people with opportunities to describe and reflect on their own experiences and perspectives. A general statement by the facilitator contextualizing and framing the issue should be followed by a series of *focus questions* similar in format to those provided for individual interviews:

> **Grand tour questions.** These questions enable people to express their experience and perspectives in their own terms: "We're meeting today to think about ways we might more effectively link with families in our community. I'd like to give you time, initially, to talk about ways you currently link with families, then extend our discussions from there. Please focus initially on the first question 'How do I link currently with families?'"
>
> **Mini-tour questions.** As people explore these issues, further questions may emerge from issues arising in their discussion. "There's not enough time," "There are some parents who never contact me," and so on. These statements are reframed in question form and become subjects for further sharing of information: "What are the different ways we currently make time to link with parents?" "What are the ways we currently link with parents who are difficult to contact?" The sharing of information in this way not only enables people to benefit from each other's experience, but also provides possibilities for directly formulating solutions to issues as they emerge.
>
> **Guided tour questions.** Focus groups may engage in a guided tour, in which people tour a classroom, school, or other sites, sharing their experiences or perspectives of events related to those environments.

Task-related questions. Groups may also benefit from task-related questions, so that members are able to demonstrate how they go about achieving some purpose. For example, "Could you show us how you organize the lessons you've been talking about?" "Could you show the group how you present this type of material in your class?" Having people express their perspective *artistically* can sometimes provide very evocative understandings of their experience, and *maps and diagrams* provide highly productive ways for people to explore and express their ideas or issues. Facilitators may ask people, either individually or as a group, to draw a picture, a map, or a diagram illustrating their experience of the issue on which they are focused. These productions then become the focus for further discussions, extending people's understanding of participant experiences and perspectives.

Facilitators should ensure that each group keeps an ongoing record of their discussion. This may take the form of notes, recorded by a volunteer in the group, but sometimes may be recorded in summary form on charts. Where multiple groups are engaged in discussions, a plenary session should provide opportunities for participants to share the results of their exploration.

PARTICIPANT OBSERVATION

The principal purpose of observation is to familiarize researchers with the context in which issues and events are played out, or to provide participants with opportunities to stand back from their everyday involvement and watch purposefully as events unfold. This extends both their perceptions and understandings of the everyday features of their life-world, and provides information for the construction of reports. Careful observation enables participants to "build a picture" of the context and the activities and events within it, revealing details of the setting as well as the mundane, routine activities comprising the life-world of teachers, students, and administrators. Sometimes, however, the opportunity to observe is revelatory, providing keen insights or illuminating important but taken-for-granted features of school and classroom life.

Observation in action research is very different from the highly structured types of observation required in experimental research. Here the researcher notes the frequency of specific types of behavior, acts, or events using a highly structured observation schedule. Participant observation in action research is much more open-ended, its purpose being to provide more detailed descriptions of the people's actions and the context in which they occur—to come to a deeper level of understanding through extended immersion in that context and interaction with people and events within it.

As I facilitated the internal evaluation of BSIC, I recorded observations of the school as field notes. This information provided the basis for a description of the school and the community context in which it was located. Readers of the report were able readily to locate themselves and their context as a precursor to reflecting on the events and activities on which the remainder of the report focused. A number of people commented favorably on this process, noting the way the description enabled them to focus on the events described as part of their own experience.

At another time, I engaged in an extended study of classrooms in a school in my state. As I watched children and teachers interact in classrooms over an extended period, a different picture of classroom life emerged for me. As a teacher I had experienced classrooms as intensively busy places, with activities and events unfolding in rapid and complex interaction. As I observed each child for an extended period, however, I saw a completely different picture emerge, one composed of long periods of silence and inactivity, the boredom and impatience of the children almost palpable. I now see classrooms in quite a different way.

As with interviews, observation needs to be focused, so that only details relevant to the issue investigated are recorded. Spradley (1979b) suggests that observations should always be accompanied or preceded by asking participants relevant questions, the answers thus guiding researcher observations. A research facilitator may ask participants for a "guided tour," with the underlying question in mind "What do I need to know about this school/classroom to understand the issue investigated?" As the tour progresses, the researcher might say "Tell me about this school [or classroom, community, etc.]." Observations will focus on any of the following issues:

- **People:** students, teachers, administrators, specialist staff, and so on
- **Places:** classrooms, play areas, offices, homes, community contexts, locations of activities and events; physical layouts
- **Acts:** single actions that people take (e.g., a child erasing some words)
- **Activities:** a set of related acts (e.g., a child writing a story)
- **Events:** a set of related activities (e.g., a written expression class)
- **Objects:** buildings, furniture, equipment, books, learning materials
- **Purposes:** what people are trying to accomplish
- **Time:** times, frequency, duration, and sequencing of events and activities
- **Feelings:** emotional orientations and responses to people, events, activities, and so on

The purpose of this process is to provide a clear record of events and activities as they actually occur, rather than relying solely on participant accounts. It provides researchers with information that enables them to construct a general picture of the context in which events occur, as well as record details of particular sets of events. The researcher should, wherever possible, check his or her observations with participants, since it is easy to misinterpret what is happening. A yawn may be indicative, for instance, of boredom, nervousness, tiredness, or cynicism.

In one study I summarized a meeting in this way: "The principal met staff to present the new school policy. The faculty appeared rather disgruntled with the new policy but made no comment about it." Here I noted information related to (a) the purpose of the meeting and (b) the feelings of the staff. When I checked with the staff to verify the authenticity of my interpretation I discovered that I had misinterpreted the situation. They were not particularly concerned about the new policy, but were unhappy with other (hidden) agendas they felt to be implicit in the principal's presentation.

Recording Observations

Field Notes Field notes enable researchers to record detailed descriptions of actual places and events as they occur naturally. As researchers meet members of stakeholding groups, they will have opportunities to gain a clearer picture of the research context by observing the settings and events in which participants carry out their daily educational activities. They should record their observations in field notes that provide ongoing records of important elements of each part of the setting. In some contexts it is not possible to record field notes immediately. In these cases, observers should record events as soon as possible after they occur.

The task may appear quite daunting, as any context contains huge amounts of information that could be recorded. As indicated earlier, researchers should record the information needed by an audience to understand the *context* and *social processes* related to the issue investigated, using the previous framework as a guide (people, places, events, etc.). The recorded information provides material that will later be used to provide descriptions of the context of the research, or of events and activities.

Written descriptions may be supplemented by hand-drawn maps or pictures that provide increased clarity. A map of a school or classroom, for instance, provides a pictoral representation that may be later used to provide increased understanding and clarity. Observers may "set up" their observations by describing and drawing the setting, then recording pertinent events and activities as they occur over a period of time, then member checking to ensure appropriate renditions of both setting and events.

Photographs Photographs provide a useful record, enabling later audiences to more clearly visualize settings and events. Photographs may be used to stimulate discussion during focus groups, or provide the basis for focusing and/or extending interviews. A grand tour question such as "Tell me what's happening in this photograph" can provide richly detailed descriptions, an especially useful process when working with children. Photographs may also be used to enhance reports presented to participants or to other research audiences.

Video Recording The increasing availability of video equipment provides an important research resource. Written descriptions are necessarily limited, focusing on specific features of the situation and providing what is really a rudimentary understanding of the events and the context. Video recording has the advantage of making the scene immediately available to viewers, providing a far greater depth of understanding of the acts, activities, events, interactions, behaviors, and the nature of the context. Extended video recordings can reveal highly informative pictures easily viewed by large audiences.

Careful consideration needs to be given to the specific settings and events to be recorded. Schouten and Watling (1997) suggest a process by which participants "*beacon out*" their fields of concern, exploring the extent of their investigations through dialogue, then focusing on salient features to be recorded. They suggest the following basic procedures:

- Leave a 10-second gap at the beginning of each tape.
- Make a trial recording to ensure equipment is working.
- Enable people time to "warm up" before recording.
- Check the material immediately after recording.
- Stick to a designated time limit.
- Allow time for people to comment after recording.

Videos, however, do not reveal "the facts" or "the truth." They still provide only partial information, since only small segments of time may be recorded, and the lens focuses only on particular features of the context or events, according to the particular interest or interpreting eye of the photographer. A useful way of using this particular tool is to record events identified by preliminary analyses of interview data. The camera then focuses on features of the scene identified as significant by participants in the process.

ARTIFACTS: DOCUMENTS, RECORDS, MATERIALS, AND EQUIPMENT

In traditional anthropological investigations, understanding a cultural context sometimes requires an intensive study of artifacts related to the daily social life of the setting. This is true to some extent in action research, though the focus on artifacts is somewhat different in nature. Much information related to educational issues investigated in schools can be found in documents and records, and useful insight may be gained by perusing books, materials, and equipment used for teaching, learning, or administration. A survey of the physical facilities—furniture, buildings, classrooms offices, and so on—may also be instructive.

Researchers, however, need to be parsimonious and focused, since huge and unwieldy piles of information—most of which has little apparent pertinence to the issue investigated—may overwhelm an investigation. In participatory action research, participant accounts provide a frame of reference to focus further observation. Preliminary analysis of interview data reveals the features and elements of experience or context that might benefit from the gathering of additional information. Comments such as "I hate the text we're using. It's so boring," or "I'm learning so much more this semester," may lead to a review of texts used in the class, or an examination of achievement records.

Ultimately, however, material is collected according to whether or not it appears pertinent to the issue investigated. Researchers do not determine which artifacts are to be reviewed prior to commencement of the study, however, since their pertinence or relevance to the research question is revealed as participant perspectives emerge. Whether school grades, classroom texts, furniture, school facilities, or other items are included becomes evident when they are mentioned in participant interview responses. Reviewing interview field notes or transcripts therefore enables researchers to identify the artifacts to be included in the study.

Documents

Researchers can obtain a great deal of significant information by reviewing documents in the research context. In classrooms, a syllabus, curriculum, or timetable may provide crucial information about the teaching/learning features of the setting. At the school or district level, policy documents may include rules and regulations providing insight into institutionally approved behaviors, activities, or procedures. Policy documents also provide information about a school, school district, or state department. These may be complemented by annual reports containing details of the structure, purposes, operations, and resources of the school, district, or state department. Memos, meeting minutes, procedure statements, school or district plans, evaluation reports, press accounts, public relations materials, information statements, and newsletters likewise extend understanding about a school's organization and operation. Researchers should keep records of documents reviewed, noting any significant information and its source. In some cases, they may be able to obtain photocopies of relevant documents to add to the body of data.

In reviewing documents and records, research participants should always keep in mind that they are not finding "the facts" or "the truth." Information is always influenced by the authors or written in accordance with particular people's motives, agendas, and perspectives. This is as true at the organizational level as it is at the level of the individual, since people or groups in positions of influence and power are able to inscribe their perspective, values, and biases into official documents and records. Documents and records, therefore, should always be viewed as just information from another source or stakeholder, having no more legitimacy or "truth value" than that of any other stakeholder.

Records

Confidential records often are not available for public scrutiny, and researchers may need special circumstances and appropriate formal approval to gain access to them. Where research is "in-house," however, review of records can often provide invaluable information. Individual records of student behavior and achievement, school records of student numbers and attendance, and district or state records may provide information central to the investigation. Comparisons with other students, classes, or schools often reveal interesting information that provides a much-needed perspective to an investigation. Perceptions that a school is poorly funded or that achievement levels are low may not be borne out by a review of the records of other schools in a district or state. As with all information, however, such information needs to be carefully evaluated, since much of it is recorded in a statistical form that requires careful interpretation. In circumstances where statistical information is used, the research team needs to include someone with the relevant expertise to interpret the information acquired. Figure 3 lists types of documents and records.

Student Work Samples

Student work samples provide a wonderful resource for investigation, providing highly informative, concrete visual information. They enable research participants to gain rich understandings of the types of activity in which children have engaged in classrooms, or lesson plans and syllabi used by teachers in formulating teaching/learning processes. Work samples provide useful material when constructing reports, enabling audiences direct access to the outcomes of people's activities. As with documents, however, they should be collected parsimoniously, since they tend to accumulate with astonishing speed. Work samples should be gathered once preliminary analysis of interview data provides a focus for selection.

As with participant sampling, work samples may be selected to demonstrate:

- variation in student work.
- extreme examples of student work.
- typical student work.
- student work that exhibits particular characteristics.
- exceptional cases of student work.

As with other artifacts, student work samples should be selected according to their relevance to the research issue, as becomes evident in the course of interviews with participants.

Lesson plans	Research reports
Syllabi	Demographics
Curricula	Statistics
Projects	Databases
Assignments	
Timetables	Legislation
	Rules and regulations
Grades	Policies and procedures
Achievement records	Annual reports
Work portfolios	Budgets
Attendance records	Archives
Report cards	
Case records	Constitutions
	Meeting minutes and
Books	agendas
Texts	Rosters
Book lists	Correspondence
Reading lists	Email
Bibliographies	Memos
	Reports
Diaries	
Calendars	Circulars
Phone logs	Notice boards
Schedules	Pamphlets and brochures
Appointment books	Lecture notes
Mileage records	

Figure 3
Documents and Records

Materials, Equipment, and Facilities

A review of material and equipment (see Figure 4) provides useful input to the investigation, since education is affected by a vast array of artifacts that influence events in classrooms and schools. Books, stationery, storage space, furniture, laboratory equipment, computers, art equipment, music materials and instruments, physical education equipment, play space and equipment, buildings, rooms, offices, and so on, may all have a significant effect on schooling. Students and schools may, for instance, be hampered by lack of equipment or by facilities in a poor state of repair. Research participants should carefully review these types of items, in conjunction with other data gathering processes. As with other observations, the focus and direction of reviews will depend, to a large extent, on information acquired in interviews.

Recording Information

As researchers review artifacts they should take careful note of information they consider relevant to the investigation. They should list information they have reviewed, together

Newspapers	Rooms	Books
Journal articles	Space arrangements	Texts
Magazines	Lighting	Artwork
Television reports	Ventilation	Craftwork
and documentaries	Air conditioning	Student work
Radio	Heating	
Films		Art materials
Photos		Craft materials
Maps		
Posters		Furniture
		Computers
		Televisions
		Projectors

Figure 4
Materials, Equipment, and Facilities

One of the best schools for Aboriginal children I have observed was also the poorest, in material terms. Despite the dilapidated furniture, obsolete texts, and paucity of materials, the school rang with the life and vitality of the children and parents who participated in its programs in an ongoing way. It made me rethink my cherished notions about what was necessary for an adequate education for children. Sometimes in focusing on the material artifacts of schooling, we miss important truths about the emotional, intellectual, and spiritual features of people's experience. Observations need to be treated warily as a source of understanding.

On the other hand, teacher perceptions of deficiencies in teaching and learning materials in a recent school evaluation were confirmed by a review of that school's inventory. Triangulation, the comparing of different sources of data, can greatly enhance participant perspectives.

with a summary description of the nature of the material. In the process, they should record which information may be made public and which must be kept confidential. The intent of the summaries is to provide stakeholders with information about materials that might enhance their investigation. If, for instance, stakeholders have a perception that student achievement levels are declining, then access to appropriate records will enable them to check whether or not this is so. This information will enable participants to extend, clarify, or enhance existing issues and perspectives as they emerge.

SURVEYS

A survey is another means of providing input into an action research process. Unlike "quasi-experiments" that use statistical analysis to test a hypothesis, surveys are sometimes used in action research to acquire information from larger groups of participants. A survey may be used, for instance, to acquire information from parents whose children attend a school. The major advantage of surveys is that they provide a comparatively inexpensive means to acquire information from a large number of people within a limited time frame. Their disadvantage is that it is frequently difficult to obtain responses from those surveyed, and the information that can be obtained by this means is generally fixed.

Creswell (2002) describes the different ways surveys can be administered: self-administered questionnaires, telephone interviews, face-to-face interviews, computer-assisted interviews, and website and Internet surveys. He suggests there are two basic survey designs: a cross-sectional design that collects information from people at one point in time, and a longitudinal design that studies changes in a group or population over time. Surveys always obtain information about people's perspectives on an issue, rather than their actual behaviors. A study of student perspectives on "homework," for instance, may focus on student attitudes, beliefs, and opinions, or be designed to elicit information about their perceptions, feelings, priorities, concerns, and experiences of "homework." The latter is more appropriate for action research, which focuses largely on revealing the perspectives and experiences of participants.

Researchers may increase the validity of a survey by ensuring it is grounded in concepts and ideas that more closely fit the experiences and perspectives of those surveyed, by doing face-to-face interviews with a small sample of participants (see earlier "Interviews" discussion). They may then use that information to formulate questions for the survey instrument. Surveys can be conducted through face-to-face interviews or through paper-and-pen questionnaires, and each type may be administered to individuals or groups. Paper-and-pen questionnaires are useful when researchers require specific information about a limited number of items, or where sensitive issues are explored.

Questions in action research surveys may be comparatively unstructured and open-ended to maximize opportunities for respondents to answer questions in their own terms, or highly structured to acquire specific information related to issues of concern.

Conducting a Survey

- **Determine the purpose, focus, and participants.** Prior to constructing the survey instrument (questionnaire), carefully define:
  - issues to be included.
  - the type of information to be obtained.
  - the people from whom it will be acquired.
- **Formulate questions.** Ensure that questions:
  - cover all issues and all types of information identified.
  - are clear and unambiguous.
  - do not include two issues in one question (e.g., Should students be able to be in classrooms at lunchtime and after school?).
  - are framed in positive terms, rather than negative.
  - do not contain jargon likely to be unfamiliar to respondents.
  - are short and to the point.

- **Responses.** Provide appropriate response formats. Formats should provide sufficient space for responses to open-ended or semistructured questions. Questions may take the following forms:
  - **Open response:** "How many minutes should be allocated for lunch break? _____ minutes"
  - **Fixed response:** "When should children leave school after classes finish—within 5 minutes, within 15 minutes, or within 30 minutes?"
  - **Dual response:** Responses choosing between two alternatives (e.g., yes/no, agree/disagree, male/female).
  - **Rating response:** These questions end with a statement similar to: "Using the following scale, circle the most correct response 1 (strongly disagree), 2 (disagree), 3 (neutral), 4 (agree), 5 (strongly disagree)."
- **Provide framing information.** Inform potential respondents of the purpose and nature of the survey. Include information about the likely duration of the interview/session and the types of responses required (e.g., extended responses or precise responses).
- **Trial.** Test the adequacy of the questions by having preliminary interviews or questionnaire-completing sessions with a small number of people. Modify questions that prove to be inappropriate or ambiguous.
- **Administer** the questionnaire, or conduct the survey.
- **Thank** people for their participation.
- **Analyze** the data.

Where more complex, extended, and/or analytic surveys are contemplated, researchers should use appropriate sources to ensure effective and valid designs (e.g., Bell, 1993; Cook & Campbell, 1979; Creswell, 2002; Fink, 1995; Oppenheim, 1966; Youngman, 1982).

The Barrios Juntas Neighborhood Collective worked with parents and teachers to improve communication between families and the schools. They interviewed parents and teachers to explore ways of improving parent–teacher conferences. Parents were asked the following questions following their conference with teachers:

1. How do you feel about your parent–teacher conference?
2. How does it compare with other conferences?
3. What did you and the teacher talk about?
4. What would you have liked to talk more about?
5. How could teachers make your next conference better?
6. How could parents make the next conference better?

Similar questions were put to teachers. Results of both sets of information were analyzed separately using categorizing and coding techniques, suggesting a number of ways in which parent–teacher conferences could be improved. The school was able to put a number of recommendations emerging from this survey into practice in following parent–teacher conference days.

QUANTITATIVE INFORMATION: STATISTICAL AND NUMERICAL DATA

In their day-to-day classroom tasks, teachers will work with a variety of statistical information—student scores on classroom tests, state and national tests, and diagnostic tests; attendance records; intelligence and aptitude test scores; and so on. Statistical information provides data relevant to the assessment of student learning (How well has each of my students learned this material/skill?), and evaluation of teacher performance (What is the overall performance of my students?). In this era of "accountability," however, statistical information takes on even greater significance, with teachers and administrators now being held "accountable" for the performance of their students on standardized tests. Regular, centralized testing is used to evaluate the level of student performance in core content areas, and in some cases, as in the No Child Left Behind regime in the United States, punitive action is taken for poorly performing schools.

Unlike in experimental research, where statistical data is used to test hypotheses, action research uses quantitative data as another form of information to extend or clarify participant understandings of an issue or problem. Numerical and statistical data are particularly useful where there is lack of clarity about the occurrence of particular phenomena. Depending on the nature of the study, statistical information may provide descriptive information related to:

- **occurrences** of a phenomenon, for example, the number of girls in a school, the number of students in a class.
- **comparisons** of different occurrences, for example, the number of girls compared to the number of boys, or girls' scores compared with boys' scores on reading tests.
- **trends,** or **history of occurrences over time,** for example, reading scores are declining over time.
- **central tendencies**—mean score of students on an achievement test.
- **distribution of scores**—whether there is a wide spread of scores in a classroom achievement test, or whether most students have similar scores.
- **correlations,** which measure the degree of relationship between any two phenomena, for example, whether success in reading is related to gender, social class, or ethnicity.

The following section describes some of the more common types and forms of quantitative data that might be incorporated into a traditional action research study. Treatments of the sophisticated and complex statistics required to enact or evaluate more extensive studies can be found in a wide range of texts designed for these purposes (e.g., Creswell, 2002; Gay, Mills, & Airasian, 2006).

Teacher-Made Tests

Teachers construct tests to monitor the performance of students, measuring the extent to which each student has accomplished the learning objectives of a lesson. A well-constructed test will provide a clear measure of attainment for each competency or proficiency, measuring each of the different types of knowledge or skills described in the lesson objectives. A record of results provides the means to track a student's progress in each area of the curriculum, or to gain a clear picture of the overall performance of the class. This type of data is therefore useful for monitoring student performance or evaluating the effectiveness of instruction.

Textbook Unit Tests

School textbooks often provide unit tests that, like teacher-made tests, are designed to measure student learning on a particular content area or skill. Like teacher tests they measure mastery of specific learning goals and objectives.

Standardized Tests

An action research process might also require information available from the wide range of standardized tests now applied to students; these may provide measures of intelligence, aptitude, personality traits, literacy, numeracy, speech, listening, hearing, and so on. Standardized tests may provide purely *descriptive* information about levels or types of attributes or performance, but may also be *diagnostic,* indicating the source or nature of problems indicated by the test.

School Report Cards

School report cards provide a summary of the level of mastery attained by a student in each area of the curriculum. Information is sometimes conglomerated to provide a grade point average (GPA), indicating the average level of attainment of that student. The average (mean) of GPAs within a group may also indicate the level of attainment of a class or of different groups of students (girls, boys, and so on).

School Records

School records provide a wide variety of quantitative information relevant to the performance of students, their capabilities, and their behavior. They also provide information about classes, teachers, resources and facilities, staffing levels, student numbers, and so on.

Forms of the Data

Numerical Data Much of the data of student performance is recorded in numeric form, indicating the extent to which the student has attained the desired learning objectives. Scores may be expressed as raw scores (numbers), as a percentage, as a fraction or decimal (8/10 or 0.8), or in terms of a scale. Scores are often reported in letter form (A, B, C, etc.), but these often need to be converted to a numerical score if they are to be subject to analysis.

Likert Scales Likert scales are often used in questionnaires to record the level of a person's response to an issue, experience, or event. Commonly, an item in a questionnaire will present a statement and provide a range of possible responses. For example:

"I like the way the desks in this classroom are organized."

5—Strongly Agree   4—Agree   3—Undecided   2—Disagree   1—Strongly Disagree

Semantic Differential A semantic differential is similar in purpose to a Likert scale, providing the means for people to put a number or value on their experience of a particular event, activity, or object. A statement is presented and respondents are asked to assess the degree or extent of their response to a set of descriptors in terms of a set of polar opposites. For example:

"The book we read for this lesson was . . ."

Boring __ __ __ __ __ __ __ Interesting
          -3 -2 -1 0 1 2 3

Irrelevant __ __ __ __ __ __ __ Relevant

Useless __ __ __ __ __ __ __ Useful

Selecting Quantitative Information

The primary purpose of any set of information in an action research study is the extent to which it sheds light on the issue being investigated. If student performance is a primary concern of the study, then relevant data from tests and records may be incorporated into the study to clarify the nature of student performance. However, careful interpretation of quantitative data is essential to ensure that teachers and other stakeholders clearly understand the nature and extent of learning for the different students being tested. Once that has been accomplished, then continuing processes of investigation incorporating interviews, observation, and so on lead to greater understanding about why and where learning problems are occurring, and what can be done to improve student learning.

Quantitative information, however, is not just relevant to student learning—but it also may provide the means to clarify a whole range of issues related to the operation of the school. The information selected should be specifically relevant to the issue investigated, since unfocused data gathering may bury researchers in a large body of unrelated material.

REVIEWING THE LITERATURE

In action research "the literature" is positioned quite differently from that in traditional quantitative research, where the gaps or contradictions in the literature form the basis for the research questions. The preliminary literature review in action research reveals the types of information available in the literature that might be incorporated into a study. The literature is viewed as another source of information, together with perspectives of stakeholders, observations, and so on, that enables research participants to extend their understanding of the issue investigated. Literature reviews should be quite thorough to ensure that limited perspectives are not used as "ammunition" to force particular types of action. The voices of proponents of both phonics and whole language, for instance, should be included in any review of literature related to methods of teaching reading.

In an action research process, therefore, the literature might best be seen as another set of perspectives, providing useful information to be incorporated into the perspectives and

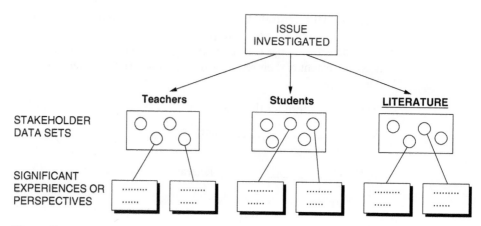

Figure 5

Literature as a Source of Information

accounts emerging in the research process. In Figure 5, teacher and student perspectives are obtained through interviews, analysis of which provides understanding of stakeholder experiences and perspectives on an issue. A review of literature may reveal perspectives, interpretations, or analyses emerging from other studies of that issue—providing research participants with information that can enhance, complement, or challenge the information emerging from other sources. The literature search also reveals the breadth or depth of the problem investigated, indicating whether the problem is widespread and broadly studied or generally nonproblematic in other locations, or poorly studied.

Procedures for Reviewing, Summarizing, and Critiquing the Literature

A variety of sources—academic texts and journals, professional journals and publications, and institutional or departmental publications and reports—may contain useful information that speaks to the issue investigated. The information may include accounts of successful practices, projects, or learning processes; demographic information pertinent to the location or group studied; or indications of factors likely to have an impact on the study. Sources may provide information about previous research on the issue, existing programs and services, or accounts of similar projects. Care needs to be taken in applying generalized information from these sources to the specific site of the study, however, since it is possible that the conditions in the setting or the nature of particular groups differs significantly from those of other studies. As a generalized set of outcomes, the results of other studies may not provide the basis for action in any particular local setting.

The literature is not a body of "truth." Studies may be comprised of a range of different theories and diverse ways of conceptualizing an issue, and may have different assumptions, values, and ideologies embedded in the research. These often-unrecognized assumptions and sets of ideas sometimes unconsciously impose a way of conceptualizing a situation or an issue that fails to take into account the concrete realities facing people in their specific situations. Part of the researcher's task, therefore, is to critique the literature, revealing the inherent concepts, ideas, theories, values, and ideological assumptions embedded in the texts of their writing.[1]

Researchers will need carefully prescribed procedures to identify literature relevant to the issue investigated, and to distill information specifically relevant to the study. Researchers should:

- **Identify key terms** that characterize or capture the essence of the issue investigated. These key terms are often embedded in the research question.
- **Web search.** Use key terms to enage in a web search using one of the major search engines (e.g., Google Academic).
- **Library search.** Use search facilities available through most university and college libraries.
- **Journal scan.** Scan the tables of contents of educational journals in the library stacks.
- **Locate relevant studies or book chapters.** Identify literature focused on the issue studied.
- **Summarize.** Record relevant material in note form.
- **Literature map.** Construct a literature map that places together literature that speaks to similar issues or parts of the study and indicates relationships between different parts of the literature. Draw a concept map to assist this process. (For example, group study that focuses on student performance may include issues such as motivation, interest, relevance, and so on.)

Using the Literature Review

As information from the literature enters the research cycle, participants can make decisions about its worth or relevance. It may provide information enhancing or confirming the perspectives already reported, or challenging the views and experience of stakeholder participants. The literature may also contain information suggesting actions to be taken or provide examples of actions taken in similar contexts. For formal reporting procedures, an extended review of the literature also provides evidence that participants have thoroughly investigated a variety of sources of information and have taken this information into account in their investigations.

Information emerging from the literature review, therefore, may be used:

- as part of the ongoing processes of reflection and analysis.
- as information to be included in emergent understandings.
- as material to be included in reports.

EMERGENT UNDERSTANDINGS

Researcher participants will accumulate information from a variety of sources, acquiring materials that extend their understanding or provide diverse perspectives on the issue studied.

---

[1] The emphasis on critique is another facet of qualitative research. Quantitative research assumes value-free or value-neutral research generalizable to all contexts. Qualitative research highlights the cultural and context-specific nature of knowledge, and the importance of understanding an author's perspective, since authors often infer truths about an issue on the basis of their own experience and perspective, and fail to take into account the often different experiences and perspectives of those about whom they write.

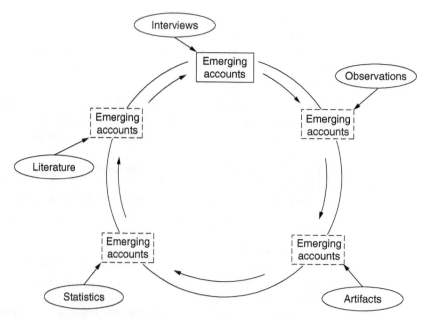

Figure 6
Building the Picture: Emerging Accounts

This information will be subject to analysis, interpretation, and, ultimately, actions to resolve the issue investigated.

As indicated in Figure 6, participant accounts derived from interviews provide the primary material for constructing emerging understandings, incorporating as they do information that resonates with the experiences and perceptions of research participants. These preliminary accounts, however, are modified, clarified, enriched, or enhanced by information from other sources. Information from observation, together with material derived from reviewing documents, records, and other artifacts, may extend and enrich accounts derived from participant perceptions. Insightful or useful information may also be obtained from the literature reviewed during the processes of inquiry.

The accounts and understandings emerging from these processes of data gathering and analysis are not static, however, and continue to be enriched, enhanced, and clarified as researchers enter continuing cycles of the process, adding further information from the same or other sources. The art and craft of research is in the skillful management of this diverse body of information, distilling and organizing data into a coherent and clear framework of concepts and ideas that people can use for practical purposes.

SUMMARY

Gathering Data

The major purpose of this part of the research process is to gather information from a variety of sources. *Stakeholder experiences and perspectives* are complemented by *observations* and reviews of *artifacts* and *literature*.

This process requires research facilitators and other participants to develop *trusting relationships* that enable the easy interchange of information.

The *interview* is the primary tool of data gathering, providing extended opportunities for stakeholders to reflect on their experience. Key features of the interview process include:

- *Initiation* of interviews
- *Grand tour* questions to elicit participant responses
- *Mini-tour* and *prompt* questions to extend participant responses
- Special techniques for *working with children*
- Use of *focus groups* to work collaboratively

Information is also acquired through *observing* settings and events.

A review of *artifacts* provides a rich additional source of information. Artifacts may include:

- records
- documents
- student work samples
- materials, equipment, and facilities

Numerical and statistical information from these sources, or from a project survey, can provide other useful resources.

Academic, professional, and institutional *literature* also provide useful information to extend participant understanding.

Identifying Key Issues: Data Analysis

From Chapter 5 of *Action Research in Education*, Second Edition. Ernie Stringer. Copyright © 2008 by Pearson Education, Inc. All rights reserved.

Identifying Key Issues: Data Analysis

RESEARCH DESIGN	DATA GATHERING	DATA ANALYSIS	REPORTING	ACTION
INITIATING A STUDY	CAPTURING STAKEHOLDER EXPERIENCES AND PERSPECTIVES	IDENTIFYING KEY ISSUES AND EXPERIENCES	WRITTEN REPORTS	CREATING SOLUTIONS
Setting the stage			Formal reports	Problem solving
	Interviewing	Analyzing key experiences	Narrative accounts	
Focusing and framing			Joint accounts	Creating syllabi and lesson plans
Participants	Observing	Categorizing and coding	PRESENTATIONS AND PERFORMANCES	Curriculum development
Literature review	Reviewing documents, records, and materials	Incorporating quantitative data	Presentations	Evaluation
Sources of information			Drama	
		Enhancing analysis	Poetry	
	Quantitative data		Song	Family and community links
Ethics			Dance	
	Reviewing literature	Using concepts and categories	Art	
Validity			Video	School plans
			Multimedia	

Contents of the Chapter

This chapter presents detailed procedures for two approaches to data analysis.

It commences by explaining the *purpose* of data analysis in action research, then presents two distinct approaches to analysis.

The approach focuses on the analysis of *key experiences*. The main thrust of this method is to identify and *deconstruct*, or "unpack," significant experiences to reveal the key elements that comprise them.

The next section describes *categorizing and coding* procedures for analyzing data. Researchers "unitize" the data, identifying discrete pieces of information that comprise interview data, then select and sort those units into a *system of categories*.

The final sections suggest how data from a variety of sources can be incorporated into a study, providing the basis for formulating effective solutions to the problem or issue investigated.

INTRODUCTION

The major purpose of qualitative research is to identify those issues or features of a situation that "make a difference"—that are responsible for, or have a significant impact on, the issue investigated. "What are the key features of the situation that affect the issue we are studying?" "How can we choose what is significant from all the acts, activities, events, and interactions we observe or record?" The process of identifying key features and selecting from the multitude of events observed is the process of *analysis*. It is through sorting, selecting, and organizing elements of the sometimes large body of information we have gathered that we are able to understand more clearly the nature of the events we have observed.

The process of data analysis requires participants to sift through the accumulated data to identify that information most pertinent to the problem being investigated. This process of distillation provides the material for an organized set of concepts and ideas that will enable researchers to achieve greater insight or understanding of events and to formulate effective solutions to the problem on which the study is focused.

The following framework therefore signals the move from data *gathering* to data *analysis*. In terms of the simple look-think-act cycle of action research, the "think" component indicates the need for participants to *reflect* on and *analyze* the information they have gathered (Figure 1).

This chapter presents two approaches to data analysis. The first seeks to identify *significant experiences and events* as the basis for analysis. The ultimate intent is to identify the key elements of those experiences and thus gain a clearer understanding of how and why events unfold as they do. The second approach presents a more traditional form of qualitative analysis, *categorizing and coding*, that distills large amounts of data into an organized body of concepts and ideas. The purpose of this process is to reveal patterns and

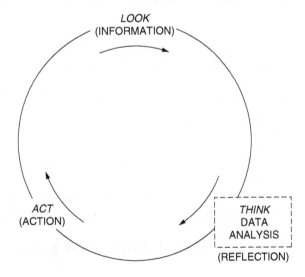

Figure 1
Analysis in Action Research

themes within the data that enable us to understand more clearly why and how events occur as they do.

Other information—statistical data, records, observations, and so on—clarify and add detail to the pictures—or accounts—that emerge from these processes.

Teachers rarely have time during the busy and demanding routines of everyday life in their classrooms to stand back and reflect on their work. Having the luxury to sit back and talk about and reflect on their classroom practices often provides them with opportunities to gain significant insights into their professional lives. I've frequently seen teachers' eyes light up in the course of interviews or focus group dialogues as they "see" themselves or aspects of their work in new ways. Merely having time to focus their attention in a systematic way is illuminative.

This does not always happen immediately, however. The students in the sexual harassment study, for instance, required an extended period of reflection and analysis to identify the nature and key features of their experience of harassment. The Barrios Juntos group also needed to work through a systematic process of data analysis to reveal the key features of parent experiences of parent–teacher conferences. In each case, however, the process of data analysis enabled participants to extend their understanding of the issue investigated, providing concepts and ideas that enabled them to devise effective actions related to the problems they investigated. Data analysis, for them, was not just a technical research routine, but the means to inform their actions.

THE GOALS OF DATA ANALYSIS IN ACTION RESEARCH

The ultimate outcome of data analysis is to enable participants to clearly understand the nature of events that are the focus of the research process. The intent is to understand how people experience and respond to the events and activities that comprise the ongoing reality of the situation. We thus employ modes of analysis that enable us to capture participant perspectives and focus on the significant features that shape their actions and behaviors. The features and elements of experience that emerge from analysis provide the means to formulate actions to resolve the problems that are the focus of the study.

In order to accomplish these goals we engage the concepts and ideas people naturally use to observe, describe, and interpret their own experiences (Spradley, 1979a; Spradley & McCurdy, 1972). As Denzin (1989a) has suggested, the focus on meanings people give to events enables us to understand actions, activities, behavior, and emotions that comprise the ongoing reality of human experience (Denzin, 1997).

DATA ANALYSIS (1): KEY ISSUES AND EXPERIENCES

Key issues and experiences are those aspects of a situation that have a significant impact on the events studied. In a study of parent concerns about formation of mixed grades in their school, for instance, the "children's educational achievement levels" were identified as a central issue. Another study of poor student motivation toward reading revealed that "ways of learning reading" were of primary importance to the students. Key experiences therefore enable researchers to understand those features of the situation that have marked impact on the issue studied.

A variety of ways of conceptualizing key experiences is evident in the research literature, each revealing a particular way of understanding the underlying dynamics of a set of events. They may be called *illuminative* or *transformational moments, epiphanies,* or *criticial incidents*, but each points to features of experience that in some way "make a difference" or are significant to the people involved.

Key experiences may take a variety of forms, from the devastating event that enters a person's life but once, to an accumulation of relatively minor events that result in problematic outcomes. Key experiences can be either positive or negative, and may include the exhilaration/despair at passing or failing a particularly significant examination, the sense of wonderment (or frustration) emerging from a particularly difficult learning process, or a sense of injustice emerging from an unfair or particularly distressing comment from a teacher, colleague, or administrator.

Key experiences therefore may vary in intensity, from the life-shattering moment of complete failure or triumphant success to the relatively mundane events that are built into the fabric of people's day-to-day lives. They emerge as moments of human warmth or hurt, or moments of clarity that add new dimensions to a person's life experience, investing them with new ways of interpreting or understanding their lives. They may emerge instantaneously—the "ah-ha" experience, the "light bulb" that enables a person to say "so that's what is going on"—or gradually, through a cumulative awareness that emerges through an ongoing process of experience and reflection.

Rhonda Petty reveals how she came to understand the concept of *epiphany*, a key experience of the "light bulb" variety. She writes, "When I first read Denzin's (1989a) definition and description of epiphanies I associated them with psychotic behavior or life-threatening diseases. My interpretation was too narrow. As Denzin wrote, epiphanies are turning-point experiences, interactional moments that mark people's lives and can be tranformational. My own experience demonstrates, however, that epiphanies can stem from the unlikeliest of sources—a book, a conversation, or the click of a telephone" (Petty, 1997, p. 76). Key experiences can emerge from seemingly minor events, and may be best thought of as significant events that stand out from the hum-drum, routine events that are of little consequence, and in some way result in particular comments or responses from those involved.

Analyzing Key Experiences

Interpretive data analysis first identifies key experiences in the lives of research participants, then deconstructs or unpacks those events to reveal the features and elements that comprise them. By starting with events significant from the participants' perspectives, and building understanding in their terms, we seek not only to give voice to the participants, but to create insights that resonate with and are consistent with the world as they know and understand it. We therefore seek emic (insider) constructions that are true to their worlds and their purposes.

We do not seek only accounts of individual experience, however, but to understand the experience of different *groups*, since individuals will interpret events according to their membership in a particular group. Teachers, parents, and students, for instance, are likely to see an issue from quite different viewpoints. Figure 2 shows how data related to the perspectives of teachers, students, and parents are analyzed and used as the basis of a report on a school issue.

Procedures for this form of analysis require researchers to:

- *Review information* acquired from stakeholders in the data gathering phase.
- Identify *significant or key experiences* within each participant's data.
- Deconstruct or "unpack" those events to reveal the detailed *features and elements* of which key experiences are constructed.
- Use those features and elements to construct *individual accounts* describing how selected individuals experience and interpret the issue investigated.

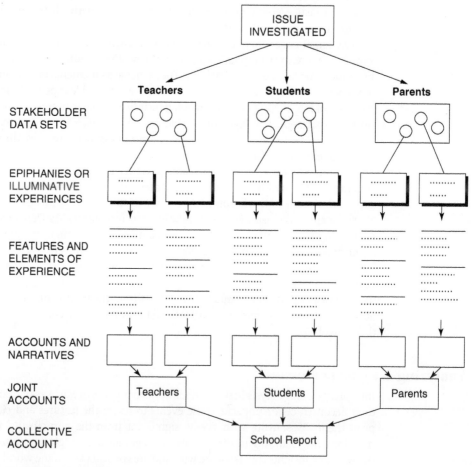

Figure 2
Analyzing Key Experiences

- Use the features and elements within individual accounts to construct *joint accounts* revealing the perspectives and experiences of each stakeholding group.
- Finally, use the joint accounts to provide the material for a *collective account*, an overall version chronicling events by comparing and contrasting the perspectives of the different stakeholding groups within the setting. The collective account identifies points of commonality among perspectives and experiences, and points of discrepancy, diversity, or conflict.

In action research, points of commonality provide the basis for concerted action, while discrepant perspectives, viewpoints, or experiences signal the need to negotiate agendas and actions around unresolved issues.

Selecting key people In many studies it is not possible to focus on every person's perspective because of constraints of time or resources. As in other forms of research, it is necessary to select a sample of people who will become the focus of research activity. When we come to the process of data analysis, it is likewise sometimes beneficial to focus attention on a smaller number of people to explore their experiences in depth and to reveal with clarity which elements and features drive events in the setting. Our purpose in selecting people, therefore, is to isolate those individuals whose experiences or perspectives seem either *typical* of other people within the setting, or whose experiences or perspectives appear particularly illuminating or significant (Creswell, 2002).

Sometimes individuals may be chosen because other people in their group hold them in high esteem, or because their contribution to the life and work of the group is seen as particularly significant. Significance is a flexible term, since it may connote negative as well as positive events and behaviors. A child in a classroom whose behavior is disruptive, or a teacher who constantly complains about school organization, may have a significant effect on ongoing events in the classroom or school. Their perspectives may be as important to a research process as that of a school principal, a highly popular student, or a well-liked teacher in illuminating events.

Key people may be thought of as those likely to provide important information, or to have a significant impact on events within the school. In commencing interpretive analysis of data, research participants will select a number of persons from each stakeholding group, ensuring that they choose people who:

- represent diverse perspectives from within the group.
- are likely to have a significant impact on the group.
- have seemingly typical experiences and perspectives.
- have particularly unusual or significant experiences or perspectives.

Participatory processes assist researchers to select people whose experiences and perspectives are likely to illuminate the complex and diverse nature of people, events, and other relevant phenomena. Even in nonparticipatory processes, however, participants may be used to assist in identifying key people, as researchers ask questions such as "Who do you think might provide useful perspectives on this issue?" or "Who in your group would give me a quite different perspective?"

The first step in interpretive data analysis, therefore, is to identify those people from within each stakeholding group whose combined experiences and perspectives will provide the material from which an understanding of that group will be drawn. The following steps of analysis provide the procedures through which these accounts are drawn, the experiences of those selected being subject to further analysis.

Identifying key experiences The next move—identifying key experiences—has no magical recipe for revealing the "true" or "real" epiphanies. Rather, data analysis commences with a process of selecting those events or features of a person's experience that are especially *significant*, in relation to the issue investigated. Sometimes they are most evident when strikingly significant events emerge within the research process itself or are revealed in accounts presented in interviews. At other times, however, judgments are made on the basis of an intimate knowledge of the person, events, and the context that comes from extended engagement. Significant or epiphanic events are identified according to the expression of the participant.

The first "reading" of the data by a researcher therefore requires an empathetic, interpretive analysis responding to the internal question "What are the most significant experiences for this person (in relation to the issue investigated)?" The participant's descriptions of events provide clues, but the complex nuances of emotion and nonverbal cues displayed in interviews also provide information suggesting those events that might usefully be singled out for further analysis. Sometimes significant events or features of experience are self-evident, with participants providing animated, agitated, or emotional descriptions of events and experiences that touch their lives in dramatic and consequential ways. At other times, a more focused and subtle reading is required to identify those features of experience that have a significance impact on the lives of the persons involved. Sometimes it is evident in the extent to which the person focuses on a particular event or experience, in the person's tone of voice or language and terminology, in the person's countenance and body language, or in the emphases given to certain events.

My colleagues and I often use analysis of key experiences or illuminative moments in the course of our teaching and research work. These provide a basis for understanding those aspects of people's experience that are particularly significant and assist us to understand more clearly the issues and events that most concern the people with whom we work.

During a recent class evaluation I asked participants to identify the most significant features of their experience. They interviewed each other in pairs, then each person identified those aspects of the class that were particularly significant from their perspective. As each person shared their experience, others were able to comment on those features that were similar to their own. Participants were able to construct an emerging picture of the class using this information (Stringer et al., 2001).

In study of health workers, Bill Genat (2006) focused on an epiphanic event within the work life of one of the participants. Though other health workers were not involved in that particular event, they were able to identify similar experiences that were characteristic of their own situations. The information acquired by exploring one person's experience provided the basis for a richly textured description relevant to others.

Key events, therefore, take on a range of complexions, both in terms of their intensity and their meaningfulness to participants. Sometimes a relatively trivial event can create great emotion, while at other times what appear as momentous events create little response. Examples of epiphanies and significant events are comments such as the following:

"If he does that one more time I'll scream!"

"Is she just dumb? I've explained it to her six different ways and she just doesn't get it."

"I passed! I passed! I passed! I passed!"

"Oh, Jane. That is just wonderful. That is the best work I've seen from you in a long time. I knew you had it in you."

"It was so important that we did this work ourselves. If others had done it for us we wouldn't have learned anything!"

Sometimes the meanings of the words are self-evident, but more usually it is necessary to provide information about the ways in which the words were delivered and other associated information. It is not unusual for people to be led to tears as they speak of events with sometimes barely contained emotion. In the example just listed, the meanings are reasonably clear, but it would be necessary for people engaged in analysis to take into account the levels of excitement, frustration, anger, and/or voice tone, such as the shining eyes and excited tones of the research participant, in order to understand the significance of the words spoken. The *expression* of the words is at least as important as the words themselves.

Sometimes key experiences are revealed unexpectedly. Many times as I've interviewed people I've been struck by the emotive force of their description of particular events. I was recently surprised, however, to find my eyes "leaking" as I was being interviewed about a cross-cultural training program in which I had been involved. Though I thought I was recounting events in a fairly objective way, I had not realized the extent to which they had moved me. The interviewer informed me that it was not unusual for people to be moved to tears as they described events within this program. I coined the phrase "ethnographic tears" as a way of indicating the possibility of engaging people's deeply felt experience within an interview.

Recently I interviewed a student who revealed, in the course of a very ordinary discussion, that she had recently failed a test. As she spoke of her disappointment the tears welled up in her eyes. She described events that seemed related to her failure and the effect it had on her schoolwork. In the process she revealed much about her classroom life, her approach to school, and her relationship with her teachers and classmates. In this case, the "real" life that existed beneath the surface of her apparently benign experience provided significant insight into her experience of school.

Ultimately, however, the choice of key experiences or significant events requires direct use of member checking, since it is easy to misinterpret or wrongly choose events in other people's lives. Ideally, when the data is member checked (i.e., when the research facilitator allows the participant to read or read back the provided information), participants should be asked which events were most significant—a "grand tour" question (Spradley 1979a) framed something like, "What, in all this, is most significant for you?" This provides opportunities for each person to identify those events most important in their lives. One step back from this is a procedure in which the researcher identifies significant events and checks their importance with the participant.

Although I focus on "events," sometimes significance is not found in a particular event, but in people's actions and/or responses, or the impact of features of the environment—physical space, dress, and so on. Significance is revealed in body language, the nonverbal communication that gives us clues about the impact of events. A frown, a smile, a look of pain or anger, or forceful language suggests the need to focus on what is said:

> "She's such a *bitch*—dressing like that and talking like that. I just can't stand being around her."
> "I won't work there much longer. The office is so small I can't even *think*, let alone do my work."
> "When I saw the work that kid had produced I almost cried. It was fabulous."

Thus as we explore people's description of events, we may identify a set of related elements impacting their lives. The feature of the experience, "The office is so small I can't even think," may lead us to explore related components of a participant's experience. Comments on the size of an office, in this instance, were related to the number and complexity of the person's work activities, and the space she felt she needed to store materials and do the work required of her. As became evident in reviewing the data, the work itself was the significant feature of the experience, even though the size of the office was the "straw that broke the camel's back" and became the immediate focus of an agitated comment. Identifying epiphanies and significant experiences therefore requires a researcher to search for significant events in people's lives, but also to make connections between related phenomena.

Key experiences do not need to be associated with momentous events. They may occur quietly and easily as people reflect on their experiences, sometimes commenting on the "little light bulb that went on in my head" as they realize the significance of something they have described. These might be more appropriately called illuminative moments, since they reflect processes of understanding and clarity that sometimes emerge as people reflect on their own experience, or hear other people's stories.

Unpacking key experiences: features and elements of experience Ultimately our purpose is to evoke an understanding of the way people experience events and phenomena in their lives. We need, therefore, to identify the information that will enable us to construct accounts for that purpose. The next step in this process is to "unpack" the key experiences, establishing those elements and/or features that enable an audience to understand the nature of the experience. We need to ask, "How is this event significant for each person?" or "What are the features of this event they would see as significant?" We are, in effect, unpacking or "interrogating" the epiphany, seeking to reveal the web and warp of the tapestry of people's lives. In doing so we use information drawn from the data, using the concepts, terms, and language used by the people as they described events, behaviors, responses, and so on—we apply the verbatim principle described later in this chapter.

Figure 3 provides an example of this process. The participant, reflecting on her experience, described how doing research had been, for her and other parents, "an empowering

In reflecting on the community-school research process enacted by Barrios Juntos, one parent-researcher exclaimed excitedly, "It was such an empowering experience!" Her framing of events as "empowering" was obviously significant, taking into account the excitement of her voice, her shining eyes, and the intensity signaled by her body language (i.e., body leaning forward and hands gesturing). From her talk, it was possible to ascertain that the empowering features of the research process related to the fact that "We did it ourselves," "We were listened to," and "We learned so much."

Exploration of what was involved in "We did it ourselves" revealed the processes of making up the questions, doing interviews with parents, analyzing the data, and writing reports as key elements of this feature of her experience. Structurally, we could map this out in the following way:

Key Experience   [Doing research] was an empowering experience.

Major Features   We did it ourselves.
We were listened to.
We learned so much.

Key Elements (of "We did it ourselves.")
Making up the questions
Doing interviews with parents
Analyzing the data
Writing reports

Deconstruction of other features—"We were listened to," and "We learned so much"—revealed the elements of those aspects of her experience. The final structure of the analyzed information—epiphany, features, and elements—provided materials from which an account of this person's experience could be formulated.

Figure 3
Analyzing a Key Experience

experience." The major features of this empowering experience, revealed in interview field notes and member, checked with the participant, were that "We did it ourselves," "We were listened to," and "We learned so much." Further analysis of field notes indicates the elements of experience associated with each of these. "We did it ourselves," for instance, was associated with "making up the questions," "doing interviews with parents," "analyzing the data," and writing reports. Elements of "We were listened to" and "We learned so much" would likewise emerge from further exploration of the data.

After having identified a key experience, researchers should therefore ask, "What are the major features of this experience? What comprises its key features? And what details (elements) would need to be included in a description so that an audience could understand the significance?"

Researchers should deconstruct each key experience to reveal the different features inherent in the event. Sometimes a single event or experience is sufficiently powerful to provide the basis for a detailed analysis of a person's experience, while other accounts may require ongoing analysis of a number of related minor epiphanies, illuminative moments, or significant events.

As research participants work through this process of analysis they may use other analytic frameworks that alert them to the types of information that might usefully be extracted from the data. A framework of concepts drawn from ethnographic observation (Spradley, 1979b) indicates the types of phenomena that might be used as epiphanies, features, or elements of experience. These include **acts, activities, events, times, places, purposes,** and **emotions.**

Another useful framework—**what, who, how, where, when, why**—also may be used to assist in identifying useful or relevant detail. In all this we are not attempting to include *all* possible detail, since the possibilities are infinite. We do not need an extended description of the more mundane, taken-for-granted properties and features of everyday life, but to identify the essential features of people's experiences or perspectives. It's important that we don't let the framework drive the data analysis process, starting with "acts" and working down through the concepts. The trigger for selecting features and elements are those aspects that are seen or felt by participants to be a central part of their experience. Framework concepts merely serve as reminders of the types of phenomena that might be included.

In all this, researchers need to focus their analysis by ensuring that the information revealed is associated with the issue or question that provides the focus for the study. They should ask "How does this event illuminate or extend our understanding about the issue we are investigating? Does it provide answers to the questions that assisted us to frame our study?" In some cases, the analysis will reveal information indicating the need to extend the boundaries of the study, or to focus on issues that were not part of the original plan. The iterative or cyclical nature of the research process enables us to build understanding and extend our study accordingly.

Identifying Key Experiences Within Observations and Other Data

Sometimes key experiences occur as researchers are observing events within a research setting. Observers in any classroom or school are likely, over a period of time, to view disruptive events that disturb the relatively orderly routines of school life. A student outburst, conflict between a teacher and student, or an altercation between staff members signals a key experience that may provide a worthwhile focus for further exploration. The event itself tells part of the story, but description and analysis by participants reveals the meanings and experiences associated with the event that have the potential to greatly increase understanding about the issue investigated. Significant events therefore provide the focus for follow-up interviews to enable participants to explore and deconstruct events and probe the meanings embedded in singular events. A single event sometimes provides more insight into the underlying structures of behavior, or the ways everyday events are experienced or interpreted by the people involved.

Key experiences may also appear in representations. They may be depicted in artwork that enables students to explore or represent their experience of a particular issue, or in naturally occurring representations, such as the graffiti that often appears on school buildings or furniture, in the form of pictures or slogans—"Mr. Jones is a. . . . .," "School sucks," and so on. While all graffiti expressions are not significant, they may be associated with particular events or people that signal unresolved issues in the life of a school, thus providing a focus or a context for further exploration.

Constructing Conceptual Frameworks

Once key experiences have been deconstructed, revealing the key features and elements inherent in participant experiences, the analyzed information is organized into a carefully structured system of concepts that assists people to clearly understand the import of what has been revealed. These structured systems of concepts not only provide a summary of important information, but also supply the basis for writing reports and planning actions.

The following outlines provide examples of how deconstructed epiphanies—the analysis of significant events within two action research projects—provided the framework for written accounts of each.

Example One
"Everthing Is Different Now: Surviving Ethnographic Research" (Petty, 1997)

This account emerged from a study of a small group of African American boys from a school in an "undesirable" neighborhood. An elementary school teacher describes how she came to understand herself and her place in society differently, and how, in consequence, she was able to explore larger issues related to minority students on the basis of what she learned in a very small arena. She uses four *major features* as the basis for constructing her account, representing particularly illuminating aspects of her experience—"Doing Ethnographic Study: A Wake-Up Call," "Contextualizing Experience," and "Surviving Qualitative Research." The *key elements* of each are used as subheadings—"Setting Myself Up," and so on. Her account emerges from an analysis of one key experience she describes in the section labeled "Doing Ethnographic Study—A Wake-Up Call." The structure of concepts derived from the study include:

"Lived Experience": in which she presents the methodology of the study.

"Doing Ethnographic Study—A Wake-Up Call:" This section presents the difficulties she experienced initiating a "minority study." Key elements of her experience are described under the following headings:

"Setting Myself Up" reveals her reflections on her perspective in the early stages of this study.

"Is This a Minority Study?—Suspicion and Resistance" describes the negative responses of some parents when approached for permission to study their sons and the feelings of devastation she felt as a result.

"Aftermath" provides an account of how she came to terms with the situation and the sense of hope she developed for these boys as she continued her work with them.

"Contextualizing Experience": "As I reflected on these events, emergent themes helped me understand the nature of my experience, organize my thoughts and think constructively about a situation that had once seemed hopeless." These themes (*key elements*) included:

"Contradictions: Expectations and Experience" describes the discrepancy between the expectations with which she entered the boys' social worlds and the reality of the events that occurred.

"Assumptions and Stereotypes" reveals how the boys failed to live up to her assumptions or to manifest behaviors her stereotypes had predicted.

"Ignorance and Indifference" describes how she became aware that her "unconsciously purposeful ignorance showed [her] indifference" to the issues of race surrounding her study.

"**Surviving Qualitative Research**": Articulates the lessons she learned from the *processes* of the study.

"Naïve Realism" reveals how she originally viewed the project through her own cultural lenses and acted accordingly.

"Support for Survival" presents an account of how others supported her as she worked through these experiences and explored her responses so that the events became a learning experience.

"What Can Be Learned from My Experience": Reveals the broader lessons emerging from the research—that policies and programs fail because they fail to consider the perspectives and attitudes of those who formulate and implement them. "In the end I realize that developing a genuine connection with someone of another culture or race requires an approach that acknowledges the person as authentic rather than as someone with quaint customs or unexplainable beliefs or desires."

Example Two
"High School Students' Participation in Action Research: An Ongoing Learning Process" (Baldwin, 1997)

This project presents an interpretive account of how Shelia Baldwin taught a group of high school students to use ethnographic methods to explore cultural diversity in their school and community. The following framework emerged from deconstruction of a major epiphany—that students could be researchers. Exploration of the data revealed the *major features* (called "themes" by the author) of participant experiences—"Getting Started," "Relationships," and so on. *Key elements* of each of these features provide subheadings and descriptive details within each section—"Teacher as Facilitator," and so on. These formulated a framework that became the basis for the project report:

Introduction: Describes how the project was initiated.

Ethnographic Methods: Describes the research methods.

Emergence of Themes: Provides a description of the major themes emerging from the study.

Getting Started: Provides a detailed description of how student participants commenced work on the project.

Relationships: Describes how relationships between teacher, students, and other participants developed in the course of the study. Two major elements of the development of relationships included:

"**Teacher as Facilitator**" describes how Shelia acted as a guide to help the students develop the tools necessary for doing ethnographic work.

"**Students as Ethnographers**" provides an account of the way students assumed the ethnographic role.

"**School–Community Interrelations**": Tells how students came to increase their understanding of their families and communities and relations with the school, characterizing the school as a microcosm of the larger community.

"**Place—The Temporal and Physical Context**": This section illustrates how *time* and *place* were important elements of the study. Both time and context appeared to affect other features of the study.

"**The Teacher's Reflections**": Reveals how the teacher developed her facilitating role in the project and, in the process, learned to relinquish control and trust her students.

"**An Ongoing Learning Process**": Reviews the outcomes of the project, finishing with the words " . . . action research can revitalize the entire learning community and can aid teachers in changing or reflecting on their classroom practices."

Using People's Terms and Concepts: The Verbatim Principle

As we engage in data analysis it is particularly important to use the terms and concepts from the participants' own talk to label concepts and categories. The temptation to characterize people's experience in terms that seem to make more sense or clarify the issue from the researcher's perspective, or to translate it into language fitted to theoretical or professional discourses should be clearly resisted. Later, when the need for joint accounts incorporating diverse terms, concepts, and/or ideas emerges, we may need terminology that allows us to collectively describe similar elements or features with one term or phrase. For example, "I was angry," "She made me feel bad," "I nearly cried when he did that," and "I'm just scared of what he'll do next" may be elements of a feature described as "The Emotional Impact of . . . ." Generally, however, we should seek terms from within the speech of the participants themselves, adding additional words only to clarify meaning or extend understanding when the words themselves are insufficient for the purpose.

Maria Hines is most explicit about her experience of analyzing data in the Barrios Juntos project. With a slight frown she describes how "I never knew how difficult it was not to put my own words and meanings in. We had to really concentrate to make sure we used what people had actually said and not put in our own words. It was *hard*."

These words remind us to focus clearly on one of the central features of action research, consciously seeking to understand the perspectives of others and to use those perspectives to formulate actions. This is centrally important at the stage of data analysis, where the possibility of reinterpreting, misinterpreting, or colonizing people's words, concepts, and ideas—taking them and using them for our own purposes—is ever present.

Data Analysis (2): Categorizing and Coding

The previous sections present processes for interpretive data analysis designed to more effectively represent individual perspectives and experiences. Another process of data analysis used commonly in qualitative research is based on procedures for unitizing data and sorting units into categories, each of which is denoted by a label—a conceptual "code." The process is very useful for analyzing large bodies of qualitative data, and is especially amenable to the electronic data analysis software now available. It runs the risk, however, of losing participant perspectives in conglomerating data from a wide diversity of sources, and of revealing conceptual structures meaningful mainly to those responsible for data analysis. Using participatory processes of data analysis can minimize both of these weaknesses.

Purposes and Processes of Categorizing[1]

The purpose of analysis in action research is not to identify "the facts," or "what is actually happening," but to distill or crystallize the data in ways enabling researcher participants to interpret and make sense out of the collected materials. Initially this involves working with data and organizing them to make connections between events or ideas, and identify commonalities, regularities, or patterns. These new ways of seeing or interpreting the information gathered shed light on events, transforming people's understanding and providing the means to take therapeutic action on the problem at hand.

The process commences by reviewing interview and focus group data, dividing them into "units of meaning" (unitizing the data), then using these to construct an organized system of categories and themes. This system of categories then provides the basis for research reports and accounts, and for action agendas that guide the ongoing activities of action researchers. Continuing analysis incorporates data gathered through observation, the review of artifacts or relevant literature, and the complementing or challenging information acquired directly from research participants. (see Figure 4).

Reviewing Data Sets

Stakeholders in action research usually comprise groups having different roles within the context and, in consequence, experiencing events in different ways. In schools, for instance, teachers often experience and interpret events quite differently from students or administrators.

---

[1]Harry Wolcott (1994) suggests description, analysis, and interpretation as the three purposes of data analysis, the latter being generalized as theorizing not specifically relevant to the context at hand. The type of analysis presented herein makes no distinction between analysis and interpretation, as Harry depicts them. The purposes of action research require "theorizing" or "interpretation" that makes sense from the perspective of participants. Generalized theory, more relevant to theory building in the academic disciplines, has less relevance to our current purposes, though it often assists in framing the study. Shirley Bryce Heath (1983), for instance, used ethnographic methods for studying children's language use in different communities. Both data gathering and analysis were affected by understandings about the types of things associated with or affecting children's language, resulting in descriptions of the communities and the people. The "interpretive lens" filtering information was that provided by sociolinguistics.

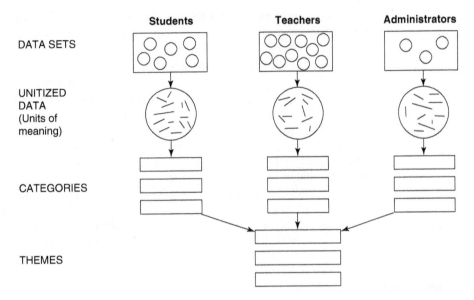

Figure 4
Categorizing and Coding

Male teachers may have a different experience and perspective than female teachers, and science teachers may have quite different perspectives than teachers of English literature. Experience and perspectives of students is likewise likely to differ according to their age, family background, religion, race, ethnicity, and so on.

Often these differences in experience or perspective will become apparent in the course of the study, but one of the important features of research is that we don't assume differences, allowing them to emerge in the course of data analysis. Generally, however, we formulate data sets to acknowledge the important distinctions existing between stakeholders in a setting. This allows us to take account of the differences in perspective and experience of the types of people inhabiting the context of the study. In Figure 4, for instance, data from students, teachers, and administrators is analyzed separately, revealing points of commonality and difference in their perspective of school events and issues.

The purpose of reviewing the data sets is to familiarize researchers with the data, enabling them to take an overall view of the information so that links between items and elements begin to emerge. Those responsible for data analysis should therefore commence by reading through all the data.

Unitizing the Data

The next step in the process is to isolate features and elements of experience and perspective, to focus on the specific details emerging from people's talk about events and experiences. Data recorded in interviews and focus groups sessions is first printed and then divided into *units of meaning*. A unit of meaning might be a word, a phrase, or part of or a whole sentence. The sentence, "I don't really like the way I organized this class because it's too one-dimensional and I prefer to work thematically" has a number of distinct units of meaning. These include {I don't like the way I organized this class}, {the class is too one-dimensional}, and {I prefer to work thematically}. As indicated here, it is sometimes necessary to add words to a unit so it makes sense when it stands alone.

A variety of methods are used for this purpose. Some researchers isolate units of meaning by physically cutting sheets of interview data with scissors, while others use highlighters to isolate units of meaning related to emerging categories. Computer programs such as NUD*IST, Ethnograph, Nvivo, WinMAX, and Hypersearch are also used to engage in this process electronically.[2] Computer-assisted programs, however, provide only a data storage, managing, and searching tool. They cannot engage in analytic processes such as identifying units of meaning or formulating categories.

The process of unitizing the data results in a large "pile" of discrete pieces of information. From these building blocks researchers sort, select, and organize information into an organized system of categories that enables participants to "make sense" of the issues they investigate. The next phase of process of analysis, therefore, is to categorize and code units of data.

Categorizing and Coding

Spradley's (1979a) schema for *componential* analysis, similar in concept to analysis of units of meaning, provides a useful conceptualization of the process of categorization. Spradley's approach to analysis is based on the idea that people's everyday cultural knowledge is organized according to systems of meaning they give to phenomena in their lives. These systems of meaning, he proposes, are organized taxonomically, using an hierarchical structure to distinguish the different types of phenomena comprising everyday life. Category systems divide and define our cultural worlds systematically, allowing us to impose a sense of order on the multiple and complex phenomena that comprise our everyday life.

A simple set of common categories is indicated in Figure 5. Ingestibles—substances that can be swallowed and ingested—are comprised of food, drink, and medication. Each of these is comprised of a number of different items within the category. The category "food," for instance, is made up of fruits and vegetables. The category system is incomplete,

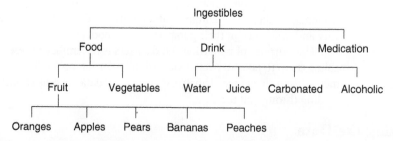

Figure 5
Category System for Ingestibles

---

[2] Reviews of these programs may be found at *http://www.sagepub.com*.

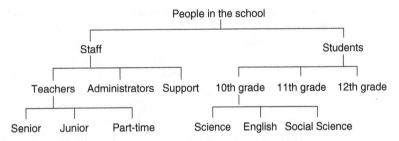

Figure 6
Taxonomy of School People

but provides an illustration of the way people organize phenomena in order to assist them to define and communicate objects.

Systems of meaning are inherent in every culture, and one of the early tasks in the life of a baby is to learn to understand the different types of people with whom he or she comes into contact, distinguishing "mother" from "father" from siblings and so on. The research act requires participants to uncover the systems of meaning inherent in people's way of defining their experience, and to formulate new ways of organizing that information to extend understanding of that experience.

Having identified the units of meaning inherent in the interview data, researchers will then identify those associated with each other and that might therefore be included in the same category. The example in Figure 6 provides a way of categorizing the different types of people in a school.

In Figure 6's taxonomy, two major types of people are identified from the data—staff and students. Different types of staff include "teachers," "administrators," and "support staff." Important distinctions between "teachers" are made by participants according to whether they are classified as "senior," "junior," or "part-time." As the system of categories is organized, decisions must be made about the placement of each item into a particular category or subcategory. In this example, there may be a need to decide whether a senior teacher who has administrative duties is classified as a teacher or administrator. Items are placed within particular categories or subcategories according to a system of *inclusion*, based on the *attributes* of each element. The categories "senior" and "junior" teacher, for instance, are first identified by asking *structural questions* that identify who should be placed in each category (e.g., "Can you name all the senior teachers in the school?" "Who are the junior teachers?").

We extend our understanding of the reason for placing people into particular categories by asking *attribute questions* that identify the reason for placing a person in a particular category (e.g., "What is a 'senior' teacher?"). Answers to these questions would provide the criteria employed for making a decision to define a teacher as "senior" as opposed to "junior" or "part-time." A senior teacher might be identified, according to the system of meanings used in this school, as one who:

- has been at the school for more than four years.
- is a full-time teacher.
- has some leadership responsibilities.

These *attributes* define a "senior teacher" and allow researchers to make decisions about which types of teachers are to be included in that category.

When we place phenomena into a category, one of the principal tasks is to name that category to identify the type of phenomena it contains. Apples, pears, and oranges might be identified as "fruit," for instance. This process is called "coding," so that the term used to name the category is called, by some researchers, the *code* for the category. Spradley uses the word *cover term* to refer to the code. Researchers should first determine whether an existing term occurs naturally in the language or talk of the people from whom the information has been acquired. Otherwise, they should provide a label for the category that clearly identifies the nature of the category. "Fooling around," "sitting still," "working conscientiously," and "talking loudly," for instance, might be identified by the code or cover term "student behaviors."

As information is placed in categories, we therefore become aware of the need to define more clearly the meanings intended by research participants in order to understand how the word or phrase is being used, and whether it should be included in one category or another. The codes or cover terms will eventually provide a structured set of categories that assists us to organize and make meaning of the experiences of diverse groups of people. The system of categories also provides a framework of events, activities, behaviors, and materials that assists in understanding events and formulating actions to deal with those events.

Categorizing and coding therefore requires researchers to:

- Unitize the data.
- Sort units into categories.
- Divide categories into subcategories, where appropriate.
- Code each category using a cover term expressing the type or nature of information in the category or subcategory.
- Identify the attributes defining each category or subcategory.

Other formats for coding and categorizing data may be found in Bogdan and Biklen (1992); Creswell (2002); and Arhar, Holly, and Kasten (2000). These provide detailed instructions for developing descriptions and representing findings.

Organizing a Category System

As researchers formulate categories they first place them in an organized system that identifies features and elements of experience in ways that clarify the relationship between them. Categories do not fall automatically into a structure or system, and descisions must be made about which categories are given priority, and where they are placed in relation to each other. In the school evaluation project featured in Figure 7, major categories identified included "Administrator Perspectives," "Teacher Perspectives," and "Student Perspectives," each containing subcategories revealing different elements of those perspectives. "Teacher Perspectives" included subcategories "Student Achievement," "Relationships with Students," "Inquiry Curriculum," and "Learning Resources." Details within those subcategories were comprised of units of meaning revealing people's experiences or perspectives of those issues. Note that there is no right way of organizing the data. It might as easily have been organized with "Student Achievement" as a major category, and administrator, student, and teacher perspectives presented as subcategories. The general process is depicted in Figure 7's concept map.

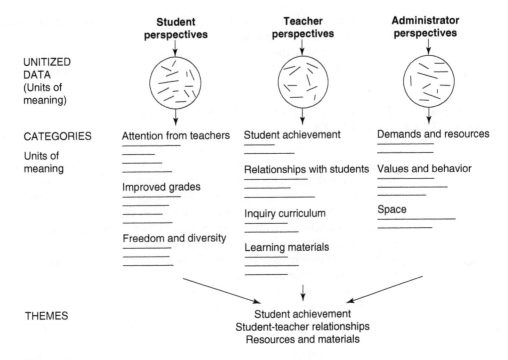

Figure 7
A Category System for a School Evaluation

In Figure 7, different categories of experience and perception have emerged for students, teachers, and administrators. The first cluster of units of meaning is labeled "Attention from Teachers," the next is "Improved Grades," and the final category emerges as "Freedom and Diversity." Teacher categories (i.e., labels chosen to characterize the clustered units of meaning) include "Student Achievement," "Relationships with Students," "Inquiry Curriculum," and "Learning Resources." Categories of experience and perception associated with administrators include "Demands and Resources," "Values and Behavior," and "Space." Although category labels provide no common elements across stakeholding groups, it is clear that some issues are related, and these have been identified as *themes*, each identified by a "code." The student category "Improved Grades" has been associated with teacher category "Student Achievement" and identified as a theme coded "Student Achievement." The categories "Attention from Teachers" and "Relationships with Students" have been linked as a theme having the code "Student–Teacher Relationships." Teacher and administrator categories, "Materials," "Demands and Resources," and "Space," have been linked under the code "Resources and Materials."

This system of categories provides useful information about the types of people whose perspective are presented, the issues concerning them, and the relationship between some of those issues. The way of organizing these categories into a framework assists to clarify the significant features of experience emerging in the process of investigation. At a later stage, they also provide the agenda for planning actions related to those agendas.

Researchers therefore construct a system of categories and subcategories that organizes the emerging information in ways that "make sense" to the participants. This is done by using terms or "codes" they recognize as representing or encompassing their experiences and perspectives, but providing new, interesting, and clarifying ways of organizing data.

DATA-DRIVEN DECISIONS: INCORPORATING QUANTITATIVE DATA

The research processes focus largely on discovering why and how events occur as they do. In order to understand the genesis of poor performance or problematic behavior, action research focuses on a broad range of possibilities, and seeks to understand how and why students or other stakeholders act or perform as they do.

As teachers focus on classroom problems and participants express their viewpoints and perspectives, matters of fact emerge that sometimes require the types of specific numerical and statistical information available. These can provide "hard" data that is less likely to be subject to participant impressions, biases, opinions, or fears. They provide useful information that increases participant understanding of the nature of events studied. In a previous example, for instance, parent fears for the educational attainment of their children were shown to be groundless by providing them with analyses that had emerged from a variety of studies. Teachers, likewise, may intuitively feel that student learning is improving, but they can demonstrate that improvement by examining the results of tests.

Data analysis and interpretation of results therefore provide useful information that can enhance an action research process by clearly demonstrating outcomes that can be recorded in numerical form. When matters of fact are at stake, statistical data can provide the basis for decisions about teaching and learning that are at the heart of classroom life. They can also provide information that helps schools determine the issues related to the operation of the school, providing data that, in like manner, assists participants to clarify their understanding of the situation and to make appropriate decisions in relation to the issue investigated.

The following statements provide cues to the type of quantitative information that should be part of a study:

- Children in this class/school can't read as well as they used to.
- This teaching strategy worked really well according to test results.
- Our library is poorly stocked with good reading material.
- More students have dropped out this year than in previous years.
- Absenteeism has increased since the introduction of the new rules.
- We don't spend as much time on math as we should.

Each of these statements requires validation by reviewing or collecting appropriate statistics. The level of children's reading would need to be compared with past records; an accounting of reading materials in the library must be made; student drop-out rates from the current year would need to be compared with previous years; and so on.

Note that the numbers themselves do not provide the final "proof" that the statement is true or false, since interpretation is built into each statement. What counts as "reading well" will affect the data gathered; the test results may have little to do with the particular teaching strategy used; what counts as "good" reading material is likewise open to interpretation; an increase in absenteeism may be due to causes unrelated to the new rules; and so on.

Nevertheless, quantitative data provides useful information that improves participant understanding of the nature of events studied and enhances their ability to make decisions related to actions likely to lead to an effective research outcome.

Presenting Data: Frequency Distributions and Graphs

When a test is administered, scores of each student may be presented as a *frequency distribution* that provides information about the number of students who have scored at specified levels. Thus scores on a test may be tabulated as follows:

Score (%)	Frequency
80	1
81	2
82	3
83	5
84	8
85	6
86	3
87	2
88	2
89	1
90	1

Total = 34 students

These scores may be placed in a graph that gives a visual representation of the distribution of scores. The bar graph in Figure 8 informs us that two students achieved a score of 81, three students scored 83, five students scored 83, and so on.

Graphs are often "smoothed out" and presented as a curved distribution. The graph in Figure 8 would be presented in the form of a frequency distribution as shown in Figure 9.

Graphs are not always symmetrical and often are skewed in one direction or the other, indicating a preponderance of high or low scores (Figure 10).

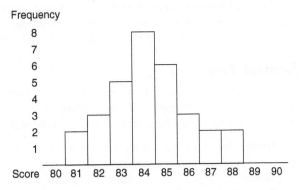

Figure 8
Frequency Distribution: Bar Graph

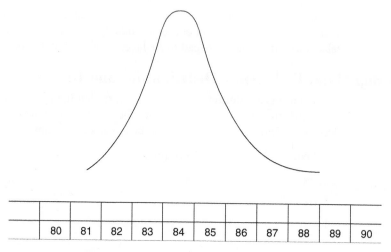

Figure 9
Frequency Distribution: Curved Graph

Figure 10
Positively and Negatively Skewed Graphs

A pie graph also provides the means to present numerical data, and is especially useful as a visual representation of proportions or percentages. A pie graph is a useful way of presenting information to groups of research participants. The pie graph in Figure 11 indicates the ethnic makeup of a school, showing the percentage of students from each group.

Measures of Central Tendency

Teachers, parents, and administrators often wish to gain an overall estimate of the quality of performance of a group of students. Technically, they may achieve this estimate in three ways—the mode, the median, and the mean. These may simply be envisaged as:

Mode—the score that occurs most frequently in a particular group. In the bar graph in Figure 8, the mode would be a score of 84.
Median—the middle score, above and below which 50% of scores will lay. In Figure 8 the median would also be at score 84.

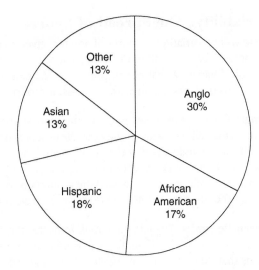

Figure 11
Frequency Distribution: Pie Graph

Mean—This is the arithmetic average of all scores, gained by summing all scores and dividing by the number of scores. This is the most frequently used measure of central tendency, providing, for example, an indication of the "average" score attained on a test, or the "average" level of staffing in schools in a district. For the distribution of scores shown in Figure 8, the mean score would be calculated in the following manner:

Score (%)		Frequency (No. of students with this score)		Sum of Each Score
80	×	1	=	80
81	×	2	=	162
82	×	3	=	246
83	×	5	=	415
84	×	8	=	672
85	×	6	=	510
86	×	3	=	258
87	×	2	=	174
88	×	2	=	176
89	×	1	=	89
90	×	1	=	90

Sum of all scores = 2,872
Divided by number of scores = 34
Mean = 85.5

Measures of Variability: The Spread of Scores

There will be variation in scores of any test given to a group of students. While the reason for these differences will not be clear, statistical information provides a clear picture of the degrees of variation that occur, providing teachers and administrators with useful indicators of levels of attainment within a class or group.

Range The *range* of scores refers to the highest and lowest scores that provide the range within which all scores lie. In the example of scores from Figure 8, the range of scores is 80% to 90%, which indicates that the group of students has scored very well. The range must be treated with caution, however, since one student with a very high or low score can give quite an incorrect indication of how well the group performed. If one student in our example had scored 40%, the range of 40% to 80% would have provided a quite different picture.

Percentile ranks The *percentile rank* indicates the percentage of scores that fall at or below a given score. If a student's score is 65 and corresponds to a percentile rank of 80, this means that 80% of scores in the distribution are 65 or lower. In this case the student may be unhappy with the raw score (65), feeling that she or he has done poorly, but will be much happier to know he or she has done as well or better than 80% of classmates.

Standard deviation The *standard deviation* describes the spread of scores across a group or population. It can be thought of as the average deviation of scores from the mean score of the group. A high standard deviation indicates that there is, overall, a wide spread of scores in the group. A low standard deviation indicates that student scores do not vary greatly across the group—that they cluster closely to the mean.

Normal distribution Student scores on standardized tests may be compared with a set of scores that provide an indication of how their set of scores compares with those of a large population. Graphs in standardized tests typically have a characteristic "bell curve" shape, representing, for example, the distribution of many human attributes—height, weight, and so on. Height is a good example. If we were to graph the distribution of people's height across a large population we would see very few adult people who are less than 4 feet tall, quite a number who are around 5 feet tall, many who are around 5 feet 6 inches, fewer who are around 6 feet tall, and very few who are 7 feet or over (see Figure 12).

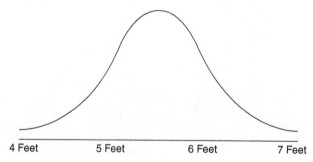

Figure 12
Normal Distribution Curve

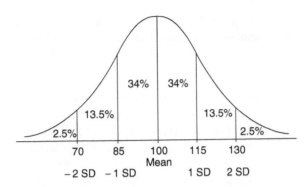

Figure 13

Standard Deviations Within a Normal Distribution

A normal curve indicates that scores on a standardized test are distributed in a particular way, a fixed percentage of scores being one or more standard deviation from the mean. A normal curve indicates that the characteristic variable being measured has around 34% of scores that are 1 standard deviation above and below the mean, another 14% that are between 1 and 2 standard deviations above and below the mean, and 2 ½% (approximately) that are more than 2 standard deviations above and below the mean.

The standardized scores on an intelligence test provide an example of a normal distribution, since the mean intelligence quotient (IQ) is 100, with a standard deviation (SD) being 15 points. Thus, 34% of scores lie between 85 and 100 (1 standard deviation below the mean), and 34% lie between 100 and 115 (1 standard deviation above the mean). Further, 14% of scores would be between 70 and 85 (70 being a score of 2 standard deviations below the mean), and 14% between 115 and 130 (130 being 2 standard deviations above the mean). The remaining 5% (approx.) of scores would be distributed below 70 and above 130 (see Figure 13).

Teachers or administrators would have an interest in these types of statistics when they wish to compare their class or their school with a state or national "average." They would calculate a distribution for their students, then compare that with state or national distributions. Care should be taken in interpreting that information, however, since scores of this nature provide very limited information and can easily be misread.

Inferential Statistics

Inferential statistics found in formal research reports use a variety of techniques—analysis of variance, multiple regression analysis, factor analysis, and so on—to tease out the effect of different factors on a phenomenon of interest (e.g., the extent to which scores on an achievement test may be attributed to or affected by age, gender, social class, race, or ethnicity). A wide range of studies and reports related to schooling and student learning has been amassed in the research literature, providing a rich body of information with the potential to inform research participants about particular aspects of issues they investigate. Classroom teachers normally will have little use for inferential statistics, since they will rarely engage in the carefully designed experimental and quasi-experimental research for which these are designed. Two common terms in the research literature—*correlation* and *significance*—provide a sense of the extent of relationship between factors influencing learning and behavior and may therefore have direct relevance to practitioner understandings of the research literature.

Correlation   The meaning of *correlation* is embedded in the word itself—co-relation—the degree to which one factor is related to another. The highest degree of relationship is designated as a correlation of 1.00, indicating that one attribute is perfectly related to another. Coefficients that approach 1.00 indicate high degrees of relationship, so that a high IQ score is likely, for instance, to be strongly related to scores of general reading ability. Scores close to 0.00 indicate that there is very little relationship between the attributes or variables measured. A score of − 1.00 indicates a perfect inverse relationship, so that a rise in scores on one attribute is likely to lead to an equivalent decrease in another. The correlation coefficient is the primary basis for much research, since most educational studies seek to establish a relationship between one set of variables (e.g., teaching practices) and another (e.g., student performance and behavior).

Tests of significance   *Significance* has a particular technical meaning in statistics. A set of results is said to be "significant" if it can be attributed to the treatment or variables hypothesized—that the effects observed did not merely arise by chance. A range of measures including t tests, chi square, and analysis of variance (anova) provide this type of evidence. High scores on tests of significance means that there is a strong likelihood that results achieved indicate some degree of systematic relationship—that the results of the study were not merely achieved by chance. This does not mean, however, that there was a strong relationship between the variables. Sometimes an experiment can achieve results that are highly significant in statistical terms, but indicate a very trivial level relationship between the variables of interest. In such a case we might achieve, for example, a high t test score indicating the high likelihood that there is a systematic relationship between the variables measured, but a low correlation that indicates that the relationship is a weak one.

Numbers should always be interpreted carefully. Numerical results do not always lead to a self-evident truth—whether something worked or not. I became sensitized to that issue at a conference presentation given by a teacher who had won many local, state, and national awards for the quality of his teaching. He was in the process of completing a master's degree, seeking new instructional techniques to enhance his teaching. When asked why he should change what were obviously highly effective methods of instruction, he replied that although his students always achieved high scores on achievement tests, he had grave doubts that they really understood the material learned—that they were responding to tests and exams according to formulae they had learned in class. In this case, the teacher's deeply intuitive knowledge of his students' understanding belied the results indicating their high achievement.

ENHANCING ANALYSIS: INCORPORATING INFORMATION FROM DIVERSE SOURCES

Thus far data analysis has been preceded by exploring information derived largely from interviews. A variety of other data also has been gathered, however, and these data have the potential to enhance or clarify information or issues emerging in the first phases of data analysis. Information acquired through *observation*, *artifact reviews* (test results, records, documents, materials and equipment), and *literature reviews* might be used to enhance the conclusions that participants reach and the decisions they make about actions to be taken. In the previous example, for instance, interview information related to "student achievement" might be enhanced, extended, or thrown into question by data from student records or reports. Likewise, staff perceptions about resources and materials might be given more credence or be challenged by information from the school inventory, or from comparison with district or state records about levels of resources in schools. Data from a variety of sources have the potential to provide a more effective analysis that provides the basis for more sophisticated and effective analyses.

In the Barrios Juntos school–community study, parent participants were firm in their opinion of the need for greater participation of parents within the school. A review of the literature would have confirmed this perception, since a large array of literature now signals the benefits to be obtained.

The perceptions of students and staff in the Brazos School evaluation study that student achievement had improved were verified by a review of student scores on state-mandated tests. This not only indicated increasing test scores, but showed how well the students were doing compared with similar schools in the district and state.

Diverse data sources are especially important when working with young children, who frequently have limited ability to talk of their experience in abstract terms. There are many other ways, however, in which children make meaning of their experience and communicate with others. We should carefully observe the ways children enact their work and play activities; the ways they talk to others; their drawings, songs, stories, and poems; their descriptions of events; and their responses to events and activities. These "artifacts" assist us to understand how a child makes meaning of events in his or her life, enabling us to construct accounts that clearly represent the child's perspective. If we can fathom ways of making learning activities meaningful from their perspective, then our teaching task becomes so much easier and more rewarding.

Reviewing information related to children's events and activities provides richly rewarding information assisting researchers, and the children themselves, to "make sense" of the issue at hand. It has the potential to greatly enhance the engagement of children in their learning processes and to increase the effectiveness of teaching. Analysis of these types of data requires interactive processes that first identify significant features or elements of experience, then check the ways children make meaning or interpret those features of experience. Researchers should review data related to:

- observations of children's activities, or their participation in events in classrooms, the schoolyard, or other relevant settings.

- aural or visual recordings of their activities, including verbal interactions.
- drawings and artwork.
- class written work.
- letters.
- stories, verbal and written.
- play.
- drama.

Researchers should work with children to identify significant features and elements of these types of information, constructing understandings on the basis of the way the children interpret the information reviewed.

In a study of bilingual kindergarten students, Cathrene Connery (2003) talks of the multiple ways in which children make meaning. She tells the story of a young boy who, hearing the teacher suggest to another student ways of drawing a dinghy, said "No, you're not doing it right.

You've got to go "Urrrr-Uuurrrrrr!! Aururrrrr-Aurrrrurrr!!—like that!" making pulling motions with his hands, apparently trying to invest the action and urgency into the sounds and motions of starting an outboard motor. The event was clear. What was emerging was the child's way of trying to capture that event—sight, sound, and words. We have a much clearer picture of his experience of a boat by combining elements of interview and observation.

Lisa Keck's (2000) eight- to nine-year-old students identified major features and elements of their classroom experience of art, discussing the issue verbally and drawing pictures to represent their experiences and perceptions. They used these features and elements to construct written accounts, completing a book and a mural to express their combined perspective on their experience of art in the class. As a structured research activity, it not only served to cover a number of areas of the class curriculum, but also generated considerable interest and excitement in the children.

Including information from the analysis of multiple data sources therefore provides a rich resource that can enhance a study and provide the basis for more effective action. Procedures for including the outcomes of analysis from multiple sources are presented schematically in Figure 14 though the cyclical nature of action research will mean that the revised analysis may be subject to further refinement in the next cycle of the study. The end product of this process is clarity and understanding that enables participants to formulate solutions to even the most difficult problems.

USING CATEGORY SYSTEMS: FRAMEWORKS FOR REPORTS AND ACCOUNTS

Systems of categories emerging from data analysis provide frameworks of concepts that provide a clear guide to issues on which research participants need to focus in order to formulate effective solutions to the problem on which the study is centered. They also provide

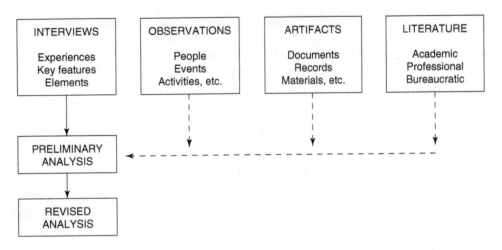

Figure 14
Incorporating Diverse Data Sources

a structure of concepts that is a useful guide for writing reports. The Brazos School evaluation study, for instance, used the following system of categories as a framework for structuring the evaluation report:

Small Is Beautiful: Brazos School Evaluation Report[3]

Introduction
History
Student Experiences
    Attention from Teachers
    Improved Grades
    Freedom and Diversity
Teacher Perspectives
    Student Achievement
    Relationships with Students
    Inquiry Curriculum
    Learning Materials
Administration
    Demands and Resources
    Values and Behavior
    Space

Details within the report derive from the units of meaning included within each category or subcategory. Thus the evaluation report includes a heading "Teacher Perspectives" and a subheading "Student Achievement" and commences with the following text: "Teachers are also enthusiastic about the response of students to the school's model of education.

---

[3]The framework for this report has been simplified for illustrative purposes.

One teacher, comparing his experience in public schools, recounted the differences he experienced. 'You have to give students at other schools tangible rewards.' " The text continues to present details of how teachers are experiencing and interpreting student achievement, including the full range of elements drawn from the unitized data within the "Student Achievement" category.

The evaluation report provided information that informed teachers and administrators of areas of strength in the school, but also highlighted some problems they needed to address—the basis for "action" that emerged from the evaluation study.

ANALYZING DATA COLLABORATIVELY

Data gathering and analysis in action research is much more effective when it is accomplished as an interactive process between stakeholders. Although it is important for people to have opportunities to explore issues individually in the earliest stages of an inquiry process, continued explorations increase in power as people participate in processes of collaborative inquiry. Focus groups provide a context in which individual information can be shared and further exploration engaged. Sharing may take place initially within each group of stakeholders, though eventually diverse stakeholding groups should be brought together to share their perspectives, to identify common issues or agendas, and to explore ways of dealing with issues on which they fail to concur.

Data gathering therefore becomes an ongoing part of the look-think-act process. As information is gathered, analyzed, and actions emerge, the process often leads to the need for further exploration or the acquisition of more information, an ever increasing circle of investigation extending participants' understandings and providing the basis for strong and effective action.

Figure 15 represents this process. Participants share accounts emerging from individual interviews, formulate a joint account, then return to the interview phase to reflect on and extend their own accounts. There may be a number of iterations of this process during an extended study of a complex issue.

A similar process is envisaged in Figure 16, where initial focus group exploration provides the material to develop an initial account. This account provides a framework of

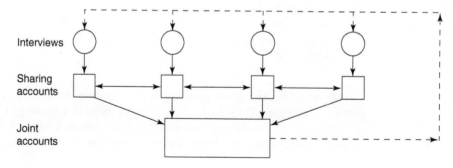

Figure 15
Developing Collaborative Accounts

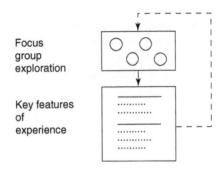

Figure 16
Focus Group Analysis

concepts and themes that is used for further exploration of people's experience and perspectives of the issue. Again, the process is designed to assist groups in achieving deeper understanding and greater clarity, providing the basis for actions that resolve the issue explored.

Analyzing data in focus groups enables stakeholders to come together to share information deriving from their own perspectives and experiences. This not only extends understanding between the diverse individuals and groups, but also enables them to construct a framework of ideas for ongoing collaborative action. As these procedures progress they trigger new ideas or memories in participants, leading to a productive extension of the research process. This enables participants to identify perspectives and experiences they have in common and assists in identifying areas in need of further negotiation or study.

Over the years I have been impressed by the amount of energy and goodwill emerging from well-prepared focus groups. Positive and productive outcomes are never certain, since a history of antagonisms or the presence of authoritarian figures may inhibit group discussions or interaction. I have experienced, however, a high degree of success in this type of activity. A recent half-day workshop with faculty within a college of education illustrates the types of outcomes possible. Faculty explored the use of technology in their teaching, sharing ways they currently used computers to enhance student learning and identifying future uses. The level of animation in their discussions and the extensive lists of useful information emerging from their discussions were a testament to their enthusiasm and the extent to which they appreciated opportunities to learn from each other. It also provided clear direction for the project team who had set up the workshop, indicating directions to take in resourcing faculty to extend their use of technology to enhance student learning.

The productive buzz that continued through this workshop was not the result of idle gossip or general conversation. As I walked around the room listening to group conversations to monitor the progress of their discussion, I was taken by the intensity of their focus. In professional contexts, opportunities for practitioners to get together to discuss the broader dimensions of their work are infrequent. Group discussions focused clearly on issues of interest or concern provide a wonderful context for reaffirming the broader contexts of professional work, taking people out of the sometimes humdrum organizational trivia of everyday institutional life and reminding them of the underlying nature of the work they do together.

CONCLUSION

Data analysis is the process of distilling large quantities of information, revealing the central features of the issue investigated. The process of crystallizing information into a category system provides the basis for increased understanding of the complex events and interactions comprising everyday events in classrooms, schools, and other educational settings. The process is not merely a technical routine, however, since its purpose is not to delineate a relatively small number of variables affecting the focus of study. Its major purpose is to provide the basis for richly evocative accounts and reports providing stakeholders with information and understanding upon which to make informed decisions about policies, programs, and practices for which they are responsible. It also provides the building blocks for therapeutic action within the research process, clearly delineating issues and agendas requiring attention. When engaged collaboratively it also provides a rich field of interaction that enables stakeholders to develop the productive relationships that are a central feature of a good action research process.

SUMMARY

Identifying Key Issues: Data Analysis

The *purposes* of data analysis are to:
1. reduce, distill, or crystallize large quantities of data.
2. provide clarity and enhance stakeholder understandings of issues and events.

Two processes for analyzing data are presented: analyzing key issues and experiences, and categorizing and coding:

Analyzing Key Issues and Experiences.
1. Select key people from within each stakeholder group.
2. Review the data for each selected person.
3. For each, identify significant issues or experiences.
4. Identify major features of those issues or experiences.
5. Identify the elements of experience associated with each feature.
6. Use identified features and elements to formulate a framework of concepts and ideas that represent each person's experience of the issue investigated.

7. Make connections: Identify similarities and differences between features or elements in stakeholder experiences.
8. Use frameworks to construct accounts and/or reports.

Categorizing and Coding
1. Review the interview data for each stakeholding group.
2. Unitize the data: Divide into units of meaning.
3. Formulate *categories, subcategories,* and *themes* identifying patterns, connections, commonalities, or regularities within the data.
4. Organize these into a category system.
5. Complement the analysis with information from noninterview data.
6. Use the category system to provide a framework of concepts for accounts and reports.

Enhancing Data Analysis
Incorporating analysis from diverse sources, including quantitative information, provides the basis for greater understanding and the formulation of effective solutions to the research problem.

Collaborative Data Analysis
Focus groups may be used to analyze data and share information.

Reporting: Communicating Research Processes and Outcomes

From Chapter 6 of *Action Research in Education*, Second Edition. Ernie Stringer. Copyright © 2008 by Pearson Education, Inc. All rights reserved.

Reporting: Communicating Research Processes and Outcomes

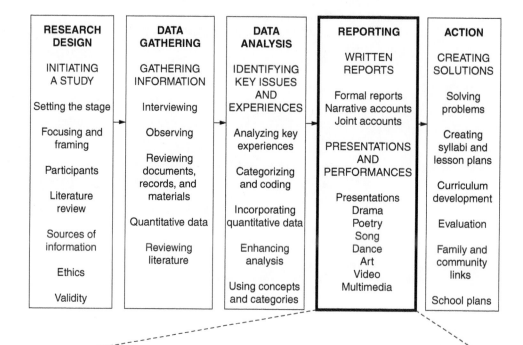

RESEARCH DESIGN	DATA GATHERING	DATA ANALYSIS	REPORTING	ACTION
INITIATING A STUDY	GATHERING INFORMATION	IDENTIFYING KEY ISSUES AND EXPERIENCES	WRITTEN REPORTS	CREATING SOLUTIONS
Setting the stage	Interviewing	Analyzing key experiences	Formal reports Narrative accounts Joint accounts	Solving problems
Focusing and framing	Observing	Categorizing and coding	PRESENTATIONS AND PERFORMANCES	Creating syllabi and lesson plans
Participants	Reviewing documents, records, and materials	Incorporating quantitative data	Presentations Drama	Curriculum development
Literature review	Quantitative data	Enhancing analysis	Poetry Song Dance	Evaluation
Sources of information	Reviewing literature	Using concepts and categories	Art Video Multimedia	Family and community links
Ethics				
Validity				School plans

Contents of the Chapter

As participants engage in research processes, they need to keep a written report of their progress. The ongoing processes and final outcomes of research also need to be communicated to stakeholding audiences.

This chapter describes:

- the *purposes* for reporting research processes and results.
- the methods of reporting, including written reports, presentations, and performances.
- procedures for developing *written reports*.
- procedures for preparing and staging *presentations*.
- procedures for preparing and producing *performances*.

ACTION RESEARCH REPORTS

The first "act" of the look-think-act cycle emerging from an action research process is a report that informs stakeholding audiences of the outcomes of analysis of the first cycle of investigation (Figure 1). The purpose of this process is to ensure that all acquire a body of shared knowledge to use as the basis for formulating solutions to the research problem. As will become evident in the following sections, action research reports are somewhat different in form and purpose from traditional academic research reports, being more aligned to the qualitative reporting procedures described by Creswell (2007).

This chapter presents a variety of approaches to reporting, each intended to ensure that participants and audiences of a project acquire clear understandings of both the processes and outcomes of research. According to the desired purposes, therefore, researchers may construct descriptive accounts, ethnographic accounts, or biographic accounts that can be used as progress reports, formative evaluations, or final reports. They may also formulate presentations or performances as alternative means of reporting to the diverse audiences that often comprise an effective action research study.

KEEPING PEOPLE INFORMED: REPORTING PROCEDURES IN ACTION RESEARCH

As people work through action research processes, it is essential for all participants and stakeholders to be informed of the continuing progress of the study in order for them to take part in bringing the project to fruition. As teachers, students, and other stakeholders engage in investigations, they need ways to inform other stakeholders who will be affected

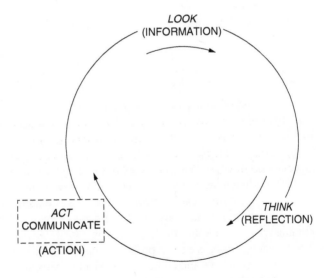

Figure 1
Reporting in Action Research

by their activities, or who will need to contribute to actions arising. If their work results in significant changes in the way their classroom or school operates, they may need to inform administrators and/or parents. In larger projects, such as the evaluation of a curriculum, the development of a new way of organizing the school, or the institution of a new program, the work will require ongoing communication between the various stakeholders. In all these circumstances there is a need to communicate significant features of the investigation to ensure that all parties are fully informed. Participants need, therefore, to think carefully through processes for recording and reporting their progress.

There are two aspects to reporting. One is to keep an ongoing record of the project, so that people can review their progress systematically and resolve disputes when people have different opinions about past events and planned activities. A written record is often a useful resource. The other aspect is the need to provide reports and accounts that enable participants to share their experiences and perspectives, providing the means by which larger audiences can extend their understanding or gain a better picture of "what's going on."

Purposeful reporting provides the means for all parties—teachers, students, administrators, and families—to understand the issues and events that affect the situation. As participants become increasingly aware of the influences at work, they are able to take into consideration the diverse agendas and imperatives to be taken into account, and to work toward mutually meaningful solutions to the problems they experience. Effective communication enables understanding.

Research participants may therefore report to each other for the following purposes:

- to share information, keeping people informed of the processes and outcomes of the investigation.
- to enable stakeholders and other audiences to understand the perspectives and experiences of everyone involved.
- to check the accuracy and appropriateness of the information emerging from the investigation.
- to provide an ongoing record of the project.

I recently worked in a school where the issue of communication became paramount. A number of problems had emerged that appeared to result from a breakdown in communication between school and home. Teachers, parents, and administrators became aware of the need to be more clearly informed of a variety of activities pertinent to school and classroom events. What became evident is that the usual forms of communication—such as sending notes home with the children—were not effective, so new processes of sharing information became a priority. Teachers and administrators found new ways of communicating with each other and with parents, making use of a variety of media, including written notes and memos, electronic mail, telephone trees, and verbal reports. These events emphasized the problems that arise when people are poorly informed. Many of the problems and complaints evident in early stages of the project disappeared as more effective methods of communication were developed.

DIFFERENT STROKES FOR DIFFERENT FOLKS: FORMS OF REPORTING

Because action research requires all participants to understand "what is happening" to enable them to contribute to the effective resolution of the issue investigated, information must be shared with the relevant stakeholders—those who are affected by or have an effect on the issue. How information is shared is critical, since it is imperative not only that people acquire the so-called "facts," but also that they understand the dynamic ways in which significant features of the situation impact the lives of the people involved. The "objective" formal reports so common in institutions often are inadequate vehicles for these purposes, often being framed in technical language that can obscure the real intent of the study.

The type of report format therefore needs to clearly differentiate between the different research audiences and purposes, since they may be pertinent to three major audiences—academic, public, and professional/organizational:

- **Academic:** University research focuses principally on the development of a *body of knowledge,* shared with a community of scholars. The outcomes of research are reported in journals and books stored in university library collections. The knowledge is also passed on to students in order to *inform and educate future professionals.*
- **Public:** Research sometimes is used to *inform and educate the public* about *significant issues.* Research sponsored by government bodies, public interest groups, or community groups report their findings in the media, often incorporating their work into television documentaries or presenting it on stage or as street theater.
- **Professional/Organizational:** Research is increasingly used for direct *professional and organizational* purposes *to improve or strengthen programs, services, and practices.* Research outcomes can be applied directly to the development of new programs and services, or used to formulate solutions to significant problems in institutions, organizations, and community contexts.

The different audiences and purposes of action research require researchers to think clearly about the types of reporting that will enable them to communicate effectively with particular audiences. These do not, however, cover the full range of possibilities, as will become evident in the latter sections of this chapter. Depending on the stakeholders, the purpose, and the context, reporting may take the form of *written reports, presentations,* or *performances.*

Written reports provide an easy means to communicate information. They may take the form of short, informal reports providing limited information, or highly formalized reports providing detailed information about all facets of a project. Written reports provide the most common medium for maintaining a record of progress or recording the outcomes of a research process. They may take a number of forms, including:

- progress reports that review ongoing activities within a study.
- evaluation reports for the use of teachers and administrators.
- project reports of classroom activities for professional or parent audiences.
- case studies.

- meeting minutes that inform participants of the outcomes of planning and organizing meetings.
- memoranda that report on current activities and issues.

There are a number of different forms of research reports, each being written for a different purpose and a different audience.

Verbal and/or visual presentations provide richer possibilities for engaging people in processes of communication. They provide more diverse and creative means of enabling people to share focused, richly textured understandings of their research activities. Verbal or visual presentations are an especially effective means for nonprofessionals or cultural and ethnic minorities to exchange information and reveal experience. For these groups, visual, poetic, musical, or dramatic performances also provide effective ways to communicate visceral understandings of their experiences and perspectives.

Reports, presentations, and performances therefore provide diverse means for administrators, teachers, students, and parents to convey the processes and outcomes of their research. They provide multiple methods for presenting new understandings with clarity, precision, and authenticity, enabling people to contribute effectively to the ongoing development of actions and events designed to improve their situation.

WRITTEN REPORTS

Written reports are derived from the products of data analysis. Key features and elements identified in these processes provide the basis for accounts reflecting the perspectives, perceptions, and experiences of individuals and groups participating in the process. They may take the form of:

- Individual reports
- Group reports
- Progress reports
- Evaluation reports
- Final reports

As Denzin (1997) suggests, we are not seeking definitive or objective accounts, but evocative accounts that lead the reader to an empathetic understanding of the people's lived experience. Accounts or narratives thereby provide insight into people's lives, recording the impact of events on their day-to-day feelings of well-being and their capacity to interact healthily and productively with the life-world that confronts them. They reveal the rich, densely layered tapestry of human experience, and the complex emotional world lying beneath the surface of seemingly innocuous events, that breaks into view in those special moments of triumph, success, love, struggle, loss, or discord that have such a dramatic effect on people's lives.

In action research, therefore, we seek to produce descriptive accounts that convey accurate insights into and understandings of the impact of events on people's lives. Writing accounts entails more than the bland reporting of events—it requires report writers to find the means to evoke empathetic understanding of the events they describe. A government report that referred to the "inadequate sewage" in a school, for instance, failed to evoke an understanding of the stench of excreta and the parents' ongoing fear for the health of their children. Objective reports are sometimes dangerously uninformative. Extended ethnographic accounts comprised of full, richly textured narrative provide the possibility of in-depth insight into the community and/or institutional contexts in which events are played out, inscribed with the history of the situation and revealing the interactional and emotional features of people's experience. Shorter reports such as meeting minutes, team reports, progress reports, and so on, provide more condensed accounts, but should still capture the essence of people's experience.

Narrative Accounts: Biographies, Autobiographies, and Ethnographies

Action research reports therefore differ in nature from reporting procedures common in the academic research literature, their purposes and outcomes being somewhat different. The latter are based on the need to provide objective, generalizable accounts that focus on the variables or factors of interest, and often sound bland and uninteresting. Action research reports, on the other hand, require narrative accounts—stories of people's experience—that have the capacity to illuminate the often complex and deeply problematic nature of events. In contrast to academic reports that often interpret behavior from within a framework of disciplinary theory (personality, motivation, developmental stages, etc.), biographic and ethnographic accounts provide the means to understand people's lives from their own perspective. They reveal the history of their experience and significant features of their lives—key experiences or defining moments that illuminate the underlying dynamics of the situation. Thus, action research reports describe events from the viewpoint of participant stakeholders in the first instance, then compare and contrast those with other viewpoints from within the academic and professional literature.

There are multiple benefits to this process, since the mere act of "telling their own story" is therapeutic for the individuals concerned, revealing features of their lives they had inadvertently repressed or had "taken for granted" as necessary though damaging aspects of their lives. Conversely, the process may reveal hidden positive dimensions of experience, enabling them to see their worlds in a more positive light or to become aware of potentially useful aspects of the situation.

The process of writing personal accounts of experience as part of an action research project is not intended to reveal "the facts" or "the truth" of a person's life, but to enable them to look at their lives in different ways—to reinterpret events, experiences, and responses, and to come to new ways of understanding their situation. Autobiographical and ethnographic accounts provide potential useful resources, enabling individuals and groups to reevaluate their place and their interaction with others in the context, to "connect and join biographically meaningful experiences to society-at-hand and to the larger culture- and meaning-making institutions . . ." (Denzin, 1989a, p. 25).

While ethnographic accounts largely have been written by external authors, we now recognize the potential of auto-ethnographies, individuals and groups working through self-referential processes of exploration to write accounts of their own lives. Sometimes, the stories are so sensitive, reaching into the intimate details of people's lives, that people have no desire to have them made public. In these situations it is possible to disguise both the people and places by use of fictitious names or by providing generalized accounts revealing the major features of their experience, but not providing the means to identify particular people or places.

We have witnessed many situations where people have been greatly enlivened by opportunities to "tell their stories" and listen to the stories of others. In schools, workshops, program development projects, and many other arenas we have experienced the joy that comes from this process. What we see is a *sense of worth* emerging from people who feel, sometimes for the first time in their lives, that someone is really listening to them, that they have something worthwhile to share with others. We are no longer surprised, but always feel gratified when people express their appreciation in the most heartfelt terms. On more than one occasion people have burst out in the moment, or quietly informed us later, "This changed my life!"

Something quite wonderful happens in the process. Not only do storytellers experience the exuberance of being heard and acknowledged, but in the process they learn something significant about themselves and their experiences. It is illuminating and sometimes revelationary. We have often seen people—storytellers and/or audience—in tears as their stories emerge. The teller does not need to be a practiced orator. Sometimes the straight recounting of events by simply spoken people—moms, old folk, children—has a dramatic impact on an audience, the "presence" of the people themselves speaking volumes. When people tell stories of their lives it is no small thing.

Joint and Collective Accounts: Connecting Stakeholder Experiences

The need to present stakeholder perspectives therefore requires a somewhat different process for constructing action research reports. Since report writers are not attempting to provide generalized, objective accounts, but narratives that capture the experience and perspective of individuals and groups within the study, different ways of constructing a research report are required. Since it is not possible to capture accounts of all individuals in a study, writers use joint or collective accounts to frame their reports.

Collective accounts are based on the notion that individual stakeholder stories can reveal singular experiences that are shared with other stakeholders. Alternatively, although they may share the same experience, participants may be affected by the same events in different ways. In writing reports, therefore, we need to make connections between stakeholder experiences in order to develop an understanding of the key issues and experiences affecting events, and the dynamic interactions between individuals and groups. Thus, when individual stakeholder features of experience have been identified, we search for connections with others. Researchers:

- Focus on significant experiences or issues for each individual.
- Review the data for all other selected stakeholders.
- Identify features or elements of experience common to other stakeholders.
- Identify points at which other stakeholders' experiences or perspectives have been affected by the original key experience.
- Record those features or elements as a sublist of the original epiphany.
- Take note of the number of times an experience or element is repeated for different stakeholders.

By comparing information within groups and across groups researchers are able to make judgments about the extent to which events, experiences, or perspectives are commonly held by those within a group or shared with other groups. These types of comparison provide information that also is important at the "action" phase, since it enables participants to identify those common elements of experience from which productive action might be formulated. It also enables them to identify those singularly important experiences and perspectives that also may need to be taken into account in formulating solutions to the problem investigated. The terminology reveals the extent of commonality—"All teachers in this study . . .," "Many parents shared a concern about. . .," or "While some students indicated . . . others were more inclined to . . . ."

Joint accounts (Figure 2) therefore provide a summary of individual accounts, but focus particularly on commonalities and differences revealed through cross-analysis of major features and key elements. Common or similar features, in this case, may be thought of as "themes." Joint accounts provide ways of presenting the perspectives and experiences of stakeholding groups in a study—teachers, students, administrators, families, and so on.

Collective accounts present an overview of the major features and elements of experience and perspective from each of the major groups, so that a school report may comprise features and elements drawn from each of the stakeholding groups (see Figure 3). Commonalities revealed in these accounts provide the basis for collective action, while points of difference suggest issues requiring negotiation (see Guba & Lincoln, 1989).

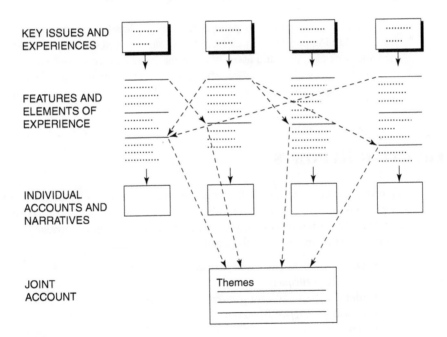

Figure 2
Formulating Joint Accounts

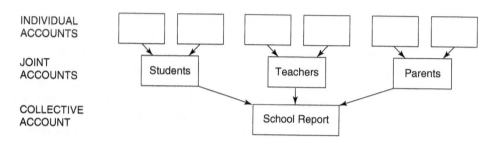

FIGURE 3
Individual, Joint, and Collective Accounts

In a recent research project in which I participated, analysis of data revealed that many teachers and parents expressed similar ideas about parent–teacher conferences—insufficient time, the need for more effective communication between parents and teachers, and so on.

Although each perceived the same features, they sometimes expressed it from their different sides of the coin—for instance, teachers felt that parents didn't communicate effectively with teachers, while parents felt that teachers didn't clearly communicate what was expected of parents.

These types of analysis provided the basis for changes the school made to parent–teacher conferences with the intent of making them more effective. More time was allocated for conferences, and individual teachers were able to implement group advisory sessions that provided parents with more detailed information. This included ways of enabling parents to understand how classroom learning processes were organized and how parents could assist in their children's learning.

In the process, however, a number of other issues emerged that enabled the school to take steps to improve the methods they used to communicate with families.

CONSTRUCTING REPORTS

Constructing effective and useful reports is an art form in itself, sometimes requiring years of practice to accomplish. By following some fundamental processes, however, most people can write a report containing relevant information and conveying emerging understandings. Those responsible for writing a report should:

- Describe the *audience and purpose* of the report.
- Identify *participants*.
- Identify the significant *features and elements of experience*.
- Construct a *report framework*.
- *Write the report*.
- *Review and edit* the report.
- *Member check* the report.

Describe the Audience and Purpose

Carefully define the audience and purpose of the report. Ask:

- For which particular people (or type of people) will this report be written? Teachers, students, administrators, parents, and so on? In which locations—particular classrooms, schools, or homes?
- For what purposes will the report be used? To inform people of progress on a project, assist them to understand features of people's experience, or reveal required actions?

Select Participant Perspectives

Decide which participant perspectives—individuals or stakeholding groups—are to be included. Note:

- whose experiences or agendas are central to the report.
- which people have important or significant associated experiences or agendas.

And then isolate the data for each of these individuals or groups.

Review the Data

- Read the data relevant to the identified participants to become familiar with the material.
- Note particularly effective quotations that illustrate key features of people's experience.
- Note the terminology and language used by participants to describe their experience.

Identify Significant Features and Elements of Experience

- Review the analyzed data to identify relevant material for the report.
- Make a copy of key features and elements of experience for each individual or group.

Construct Report Framework

Use the features and elements of experience to construct a framework for the report. Note:

- key features as headings or subheadings.
- elements or units of meaning as the content of each heading/subheading.

Write the Report

Write the report using the framework as a guide, incorporating the terminology and language of participants in the body of the narrative. The framework guides the writing process, but is not by itself sufficient to adequately capture people's lived experience. Authors of reports and accounts need to encompass in their writing the multiple dimensions of human experience, including emotional, physical, and interactional elements of behavior and perspective, as well as the organizational and procedural components. The framework that guides data collection is useful as a checklist of what can be included in a narrative—people, acts, activities, events, purposes, emotions, places, times, and objects. In all this it is important for the words of participants to provide the terminology and language of the report. Not only should they provide the wording of headings in the report/account, but their words should make up the body of writing. Some writers string together sections of the unitized data to form the body of the account. Others use quotations prolifically to clearly illustrate the points they are making or the contexts they describe.

> The BSIC evaluation report includes a heading "Teacher Perspectives" with a subheading "Student Achievement." The latter includes the following text: "Teachers are also enthusiastic about the response of students to the school's model of education. One teacher, comparing his experience in public schools, recounted the differences he encountered: 'You have to give students at other schools tangible rewards.' " The text continues to present details of how teachers are experiencing and interpreting "student achievement," including the full range of elements drawn from the unitized data within the "Student Achievement" category.

Review and Edit

Review the report. Check that:

- Its stated purposes have been accomplished: Does the report provide adequate and appropriate information to inform the intended audience?
- All relevant participant perspectives have been included.
- The language is appropriate for the intended audience.
- The report accurately reflects the perspectives and experiences of participants, rather than that of the author or one stakeholding group.

> Whenever I'm facilitating report writing, I continually ask authors the question, "Who is speaking here? Whose perspective is being presented?" It is surprising how often even the most careful report writer will allow his or her own perspective to intrude. When we write accounts we must take great care to ensure that we don't unwittingly present material reflecting our own perceptions and interpretations of the situation. The exceptions are those situations where we overtly include our perspective as a participating stakeholder in a research process.

Member Check

Give a draft to those about whom the report is written:

- Provide time for them to read and respond.
- Talk with them in person, if possible, or by phone if not.

- Check for accuracy, sufficiency, and appropriateness of information contained in the report.
- Modify or correct the report according to their input.

WRITING FORMAL REPORTS

Formal reports are those presented to professional audiences that have a significant stake in the research project and need to be fully informed about the purpose, procedures, and outcomes of the study. Formal reports therefore will be written for:

- administrative, professional, and funding bodies.
- academic and professional publications and research journals.
- theses and dissertations.

A formal report should include the following sections:

1. **Introduction**—describes the focus of the study.
2. **Review of the Literature**—presents an overview of current academic and professional literature related to the research problem.
3. **Methodology**—details the methodology and research procedures used.
4. **Findings or Outcomes**—presents an account of the outcomes of the study.
5. **Discussion or Conclusion**—describes actions emerging from the study and implications for further investigation.

Section 1: Introduction—Focus and Framing

This section of a report presents an overview of the study. It describes:

- the problem or issue on which the study focuses.
- the context of the study—where it is located and the people involved.
- the research question.
- the purpose of the research—generally, to seek an answer to the research question.
- the significance of the study—why the issue is important, or why the problem needed to be resolved.

Section 2: Literature Review

The purpose of a literature review is to summarize information about the research problem/question that has been gleaned from studies reported in the research and professional literature. It both describes and critiques those studies, assessing their strengths and weaknesses, and revealing the concepts, theories, and underlying assumptions on which their various claims and viewpoints are based. The review also points to gaps or inadequacies in the literature, in terms of its applicability to the current study. The review of literature may also point to the significance of the issue or problem as being worthy of study. The review and analysis of this literature sets the stage for a later process in which official and academic viewpoints are compared and contrasted with research participant perspectives.

Section 3: Methodology

This section of the report presents a rationale for the approach to research used in the study (philosophical assumptions) and describes in detail the people involved (sample), the context in which it takes place (site), and the procedures used to conduct the research (research methods). It informs readers of why this approach to research is appropriate to the issue investigated and indicates steps taken to ensure the study was rigorous and ethical. In doing so it may cite sources that enhance the legitimacy of the study (e.g., Denzin & Lincoln, 2005; Lincoln & Guba, 1985; Reason & Bradbury, 2007).

Section 4: Research Outcomes/Findings

Section 4 is sometimes described as the "results" section of the report, enabling researchers to present what they have discovered in their investigation. It presents detailed accounts that describe the nature of the problem from the perspective of different stakeholders, including the events, behaviors, or responses having a significant effect on the issue investigated. These accounts not only identify the factors affecting the issue, but describe the dynamics of the situation in which they emerge.

The "what, who, how, where, when, why" framework is a useful tool for capturing these issues. This framework triggers report writers to identify: *what* the key events are; *who* is involved; *how, when,* and *where* these events unfold; *why* they occur as they do; and *how* they are experienced by different stakeholders. The intent is to provide readers with an empathetic understanding of how stakeholders experience and interpret issues and events surrounding the research problem, and the effect that has on their activities and behaviors.

The following list provides another useful conceptual framework to assist report writers:

- **Actors:** The people who are significant or relevant to the story.
- **Acts and activities:** The things people do; activities in which they engage.
- **Events:** Significant events or incidents that take place.
- **Place:** Where those activities or events take place.
- **Time:** When events occur and for how long.
- **Purpose:** What people are trying to accomplish; why they do what they do.
- **Emotion:** How participants feel about what happens; how they respond.
- **Objects:** Buildings, goods, materials, clothes, cars, books, reports, and so on.

The report will also describe solutions to the research problem formulated by participants, the way those solutions were implemented, and the effect of those solutions.

Accounts should provide sufficient material to enable intended audiences to understand the experience and perspectives of key people in the primary stakeholding groups, as well as information incorporated from other data sources. A report of an investigation of school dropouts not only would focus on the perspectives and experiences of students who left school early, but also should provide an understanding of the perspectives of peers, teachers, parents, school administrators, and others having a stake in the issue, and incorporate statistical information that indicates relevant information from school records—numbers of school dropouts in current and previous years, absenteeism, levels of educational attainment, and so on.

Section 5: Conclusion—Discussion of Findings

The final section places the results in a broader context. This is the "so what" section of a formal report or dissertation that enables writers to articulate newly emerging understandings of the issue and to compare and contrast them with perspectives that exist in the academic literature or in department/agency reports. In effect, it presents succinctly what has been discovered and explores the implications of those findings. This section does the following:

- summarizes the outcomes of the study.
- places stakeholder viewpoints in the broader social context of the issue by comparing and contrasting their perspectives with those presented within the literature.
- explores the implications of the study for practices, policies, programs, and services.
- suggests actions that may be initiated or extended, or modifications of activities and/or procedures that will improve existing practices, programs, or services.
- suggests the need for further research to enhance or extend the outcomes of the current study.

The overall purpose of this section is to show clearly how stakeholder perspectives illuminate the issue investigated and to suggest the changes in practices, programs, and services implied by the outcomes of the research. In the academic world, it may also propose ways that existing theoretical perspectives are enhanced or challenged by the new understandings emerging from the research process.

A report on an action research study of parent involvement in schools included the perspectives of parents, teachers, principals, superintendents, and personnel from the education agency. The report presented the perspective of each of these stakeholding groups, and included a wide range of possibilities for ways in which parents could participate in the schools to enhance their children's education. These reports and the recommendations that emerged from them became the basis for a series of parent–teacher workshops in a sample of schools in the district that clearly defined actions parents themselves wished to take in their particular schools. A report on the widespread success of this pilot program provided the means for the district education agency to formulate a policy that provided the impetus for similar developments across the school system (Stringer, in Reason & Bradbury, 2007).

PRESENTATIONS: EFFECTIVE COMMUNICATION

Presentations provide exciting ways to communicate research results to participants and stakeholding audiences. Constructed from multiple materials and using diverse presentational modes, they can captivate audiences, powerfully presenting participant perspectives and illuminating key features of the research. Presentations provide the possibility of clear and effective communication based on richly evocative accounts that accurately capture and represent people's experiences. They may range from simple verbal presentations to complex performances incorporating multiple forms of visual and electronic media that effectively communicate with a wide variety of audiences.

Even academic and professional conferences now provide opportunities for staging a wide variety of presentations. Though direct verbal addresses from prepared papers are still common, many presentations involve creative and innovative approaches that incorporate charts, overheads, electronic materials, roundtable interactive presentations, poster sessions, and structured dialogues. Presenters seek forms of communication that enable them to communicate information efficiently and effectively. These types of presentations are becoming increasingly common in professional and school contexts as teachers and administrators share information or report on school activities.

Such flexible formats are especially relevant in contexts where lengthy written reports may actually inhibit communication with important stakeholding audiences. Children and some adults from poorer or culturally different contexts may not have sufficient familiarity with professional or technical language to enable them to read lengthy formal reports. Further, written reports are often an inadequate vehicle for expressing the full range of participant experiences. They fail to convey the emotional, interactional features of experience, the nature of their social circumstances, or the complexities of their cultural realities. Presentations, when carefully prepared and authentically presented, provide the means for more clearly and effectively communicating the concrete reality of people's lives and the elements that need to be taken into careful account when taking action. As with written reports, presentations need to be carefully and creatively planned to suit the audience, the purposes to be achieved, and the outcomes expected.

A group of graduate students presented an evaluative account of their experience of coursework in their program. Direct verbal presentations were supplemented by role plays, poetry, and art. Their presentations were richly peppered with Aboriginal names and terminology, and humor was an integral feature of the dialogical interaction between participants. Not only were they able to provide an enjoyable and informative experience for the audience of students and academic faculty from around the university, they were also able to embody the Aboriginal cultural ethos that was central to the program of study they had engaged. Derived from a preliminary focus group exploration, their presentations clearly depicted the joys, struggles, and other major features of their learning processes. It provided a dramatic counterpoint to the rather soulless, form-filling exercises usually used for class evaluations.

Audiences and Purposes

Research participants using presentations to communicate information about their research will need to identify carefully their audience and purpose in order to achieve the effectiveness of their project. The major question to be asked is "What information should be presented, and how can we communicate most effectively with this particular audience?" In school contexts, audiences of teachers, students, parents, and administrators may require somewhat different presentations, since different agendas will be relevant to each of those audiences, each of whom may have a different part to play in actions emerging from the research process. All groups, however, will need to understand each other's perspectives, so that they are able to work in unison to achieve their desired purposes.

Presentations therefore will vary according to purposes to be achieved. Short, informal presentations assist participants to communicate the progress of activities to each other, enabling progress to be monitored effectively and ensuring that all are working in unison. These types of presentations will be very different from more carefully structured and planned presentations required at key points in the research process. If participants wish to inform a key stakeholding group—administrators, funding body representative, supporters—of the issues emerging from their inquiries to garner support for actions they wish to take, then more detailed and carefully structured presentations may be necessary.

Presentations will also be affected by desired outcomes. If participants wish to generate a clear or deeper understanding of people's experience, then participants will prepare evocative presentations designed to achieve that effect. Such presentations will be multidimensional, providing a clear picture of significant events, the context in which they occur, and their impact—rational, physical, emotional, and spiritual—on the lives of participant stakeholders. This is a more emotive presentation seeking to engender understanding of the dynamics and complexities of people's experiences and perspectives. If participants wish an audience to focus on more practical issues for planning purposes, then the presentation will take a more didactic form, focusing on key features and elements of the issue investigated. Presentations that keep people informed of activities in progress but require no action on their part will differ from those presentations requiring decisions, inputs, or actions on the part of the audience. In the latter case, the presentations themselves must be structured to make provisions for audience participation at appropriate points.

In recent years I was involved in a curriculum development project to institute a graduate program in indigenous studies. Preliminary research with prospective students and associated audiences identified the content of the program—the skills and knowledge required by the students to achieve their educational, social, and cultural purposes. These provided the basis for content of study, teaching/learning processes, and program organization, including staffing, budgeting, space, timetable, and so on.

As we worked through developmental processes, different means were employed to inform the different audiences of program details. A charted summary of the content areas was produced and used to talk with prospective students about the program. A flow chart assisted the planning team to work through organizational issues with administrative personnel. A series of reports provided relevant information to a variety of other stakeholders, including institutional committees and a community advisory group. These forms of presentation enabled stakeholding developmental partners and participants to maintain a clear picture of the program as it developed and ensured wide acceptance within the institution and the community.

A smaller research study at a local school developed small reports for teachers, administrators, and parents. These were presented verbally to the principal, to a meeting of school staff, and to a meeting of parents. The project was marked by high degrees of participation by parents, and enabled school staff to make changes to ways in which they communicated with parents. The combination of written and verbal presentations provided the means to reach a wide range of participants.

Planning Presentations

Well-planned presentations ensure that stakeholding audiences are well-informed, enabling them to maintain clarity and gain deep insights into the issues investigated. Research participants will use similar processes to report writing for planning presentations (see previous discussion), defining:

- **Audiences:** Who are the audiences to whom we wish to present?
- **Purposes:** What are our purposes in presenting to this audience?
- **Understandings:** What do we wish our audiences to know or understand?
- **Content:** What information or material will assist in achieving this purpose?
- **Format:** What presentational formats might best achieve this purpose?
- **Outcomes:** What do we wish to achieve; what outcomes are desired?

Planning presentations

- Identify the **audience** and **purpose**.
- **Identify participants** whose experiences and perspectives are pertinent to the presentation.
- **Review the data** for each of these participants.
- **Review the categories and issues** emerging from analysis of data for each participant.
- Use categories to **construct a framework** of headings.
- **Write a script,** using units of meaning and/or elements within the data.
- **Review and edit** the script, checking for accurate rendering of participant perspectives and appropriateness to audience.
- **Member check** by having participants read the script.
- **Practice** the presentation.

The basic outcome of presentation planning is an *outline* or *script* presenting the information in easily accessible form. An outline in dot-point form provides a script that guides people's presentations. The script may be complemented by additional material, including quotations from people's talk or documented information to be read verbatim to an audience. For more formal presentations, people may rehearse their presentation to ensure they are clear about the material to be presented and to keep their presentation within the allotted time.

Research participants therefore need to carefully prepare a script that has the following basic format:

- **Introduction**

  The focus of the project—the issue investigated

  The participants

  The purpose and desired outcomes of the presentation

- **Body of the Presentation**

  Previous and current activities: What has happened and what is happening

  Key issues emerging from research: What has been discovered; what is problematic

  Implications: What needs to be done (actions, next steps)

- **Conclusion**
  Review of major points covered

Presentations should be carefully scripted and directed so that each participant knows precisely where and when to speak, and the material for which they are responsible. Practice provides both clarity and confidence, maximizing the possibility of an informative and effective presentation. This is especially important for people who are not used to speaking publicly, because their inclusion—the effect of people speaking for themselves in their own voice—dramatically increases the power of a presentation.

Only in rare situations should people read from a pre-prepared written report. Though these types of presentations provide people with feelings of safety and accuracy, they usually detract from the purpose of the event. The written word is different in form and function from the spoken word, and people reading from a paper usually fail to convey the meaningfulness that is a necessary function of a presentation. We have all experienced forms of presentation, delivered in mournful monotone or excited exuberance, that rattle or drone on and on. Usually there is far too much information for the audience to absorb and little opportunity to process that information. Rarely do audiences in these situations gain appreciable understanding, and retention of information is limited. Presenting an address by reading from a pre-prepared paper is an art that few possess.

Members of a neighborhood collective planned a presentation to a national academic conference, a rather grand event that seemed somewhat imposing to them. After carefully identifying the purpose of their presentation—the major message they wished to present to a largely academic audience—they carefully reviewed the material they had accumulated, identifying and assessing those features that appeared central to research in which they had engaged. These features were ordered into a framework of ideas—headings and subheadings—and persons were allocated to take responsibility for the various sections. They rehearsed their presentation a number of times, reallocating some material to different people or places until all participants were clear on what they needed to say and when. The actual presentation at the conference was highly successful, providing the audience with a clear understanding of the power of community participation in a research process. The degree of engagement of the audience was evidenced by their rapt attention and the diversity of questions they asked. The participants were highly delighted by the success of their presentation, an event that further heightened their research skills and feelings of empowerment.

Enhancing Verbal Presentations: Audio/Visual Materials

"Talk is cheap" is a common saying that has relevance to presentations. Though parsimonious verbal presentations can sometimes be effective, it requires a skilled and practiced orator to hold an audience for an extended period. Interest and understanding is greatly extended when visual and auditory materials are incorporated into presentations, aiding in clarity and enabling significant quantities of factual information to be presented. Statistical summaries, numerical information, or lists of features and elements may be presented in chart form or as overheads. Charts have the advantage of providing a constantly available record of issues, but suffer sometimes from problems of size. Overheads and other electronic means of displaying information have great clarity, but can only be projected one sheet at a time, thus placing limits on the flexibility of a presentation.

A variety of visual aids will complement and enhance verbal information. Diagrams, maps, concept maps, symbolic representations, figures, and so on, provide effective ways for presenting information and focusing attention. Whiteboards or chalkboards also enable the active construction of illustrations and diagrams to stimulate attention and enable the structured exposition of a wide range of subject matter.

These processes can be presented in highly sophisticated form using electronic media in the form of audio or video recording, or electronic presentations derived from such software as Microsoft PowerPoint. It is important to ensure that these are used in moderation, since extended use of videos or electronic media can be detrimental to a presentation, creating a passive audience and detracting from feelings of engagement. Judicious use of electronic media, however, can provide vivid illustrations or large bodies of information, greatly enhancing people's ability or willingness to participate in ongoing dialogue. As a stimulus they are sometimes unparalleled.

At each stage, therefore, we need to ask how we can best achieve the types of understanding we desire. Presentations can be greatly enhanced by using:

• Maps	• Figures
• Charts	• Overheads
• Artwork	• Audio recording
• Concept maps	• Video recording
• Lists	• Electronic presentations

For some years colleagues and I have provided workshops on cultural sensitivity or race relations for a variety of audiences. The intent was to assist them to investigate ways of modifying their professional work practices to ensure greater effectiveness in cross-cultural contexts. These sessions have been greatly enhanced by having participants view short segments of a video film showing indigenous people presenting accounts of their experiences. One popular segment presents an old man talking of the time police and welfare officers came to take away his children. Moved to tears, he narrates the way he was prevented from taking any action as his children were driven away. Returning the next day he talks of how he put a piece of old tin over his only remaining reminder of his children, their footprints in the sand. This segment, used many times in workshops and presentations, never fails to evoke rich and sometimes intense discussions. It provides keen insight into the way past events continue to affect community life. Sometimes a picture *is* worth a thousand words.

For some audiences, presentations may take on an almost concert-like appearance. Creative presentations may incorporate a variety of materials and performances (see following discussion), providing a rich body of factual information and authentic understandings of people's lived realities. Presentations, constructed from materials derived from the analysis of data, use key features and elements as the basis for a script, incorporating "quotes" from the data to highlight important information. Presenters may incorporate tape-recorded information derived from participant interviews, read from reviewed materials, or incorporate, as appropriate, segments of video or audio recordings, poems, songs, or role plays. The rich variety of possibilities enables audiences of children, youth, and adult participants to fully express the ideas with which they have been working.

Interactive Presentations

Presentations are more effective when they are interactive. It is difficult to stimulate interest or involvement in a research process when the audience is passive and uninvolved. When presenters dominate presentations, other participants are likely to feel "left out," or marginalized, as if their perspectives and issues are less important. Wherever possible, presentations should provide opportunities for all participants to interact with the material presented. At regular intervals, audiences should have opportunities to participate in the unfolding presentation, commenting on issues, asking for clarification, or offering their perspectives on issues presented. As part of an "hermeneutic dialectic"—meaning-making dialogue—these processes not only enable people to extend and clarify their understanding, but also increase their feelings of inclusion and ownership in the project at hand.

Presentations may also include small-group work, enabling participants to explore issues in greater depth by engaging in dialogue, or peruse related documents or materials. Feedback from small-group discussions provides a further means to gain greater clarity and understanding, especially about points of contention or uncertainty. This points to the need for flexibility, to allow participants to take advantage of opportunities arising in the course of presentations. It is possible to turn a presentation into a workshop or focus group, so that audiences become active participants in the ongoing development of the investigation. In these circumstances time may be allocated for this purpose to allow participants to take advantage of the ideas emerging from their work together.

When I work with research groups I often have them chart the key elements of their recent activities. Each group then speaks of their chart, reporting on their progress and any issues arising. The audience is able to comment or ask questions to clarify or extend the presenters' comments. This not only informs the audience clearly, but assists the presenters to extend their thinking about the issues raised—an integral part of the process of re-searching.

PERFORMANCES: REPRESENTING EXPERIENCE ARTISTICALLY AND DRAMATICALLY

Performances extend the possibilities for providing deeper and more effective understandings of the nature of people's experiences. They present multiple possibilities for entering people's subjective worlds to provide audiences with empathetic understandings that greatly increase the power of the research process. Performances enable participants to "report" on their research through:

- Drama
- Role play
- Song
- Poetry
- Dance
- Visual artwork
- Electronic media

By engaging their work performatively, research participants use artistic means to enable audiences to take the perspective of the people whose lives are performed, to enter their experience vicariously, and therefore to understand more empathetically their life-worlds. Using artistic and dramatic media, researchers are able to capture and represent the deeply complex, dynamic, interactive, and emotional qualities of everyday life. They can engage in richly evocative presentations comprehensible to children, families, cultural minorities, the poor, and other previously excluded audiences.

Poetry, music, drama, and art provide the means for creating illuminative, transformative experiences for presenter and audience alike, stimulating awareness of the different voices and multiple discourses occurring in any given social space (Denzin, 1997; Prattis, 1985). They provide the means to interrogate people's everyday realities, by juxtaposing them within the telling, acting, or singing of stories, thus revealing the differences that occur therein and providing the possibility of therapeutic action (Denzin, 1997; Trinh, 1991). While performances fail to provide the certainty required of experimental research, or to reinforce the authority of an official voice (Atkinson, 1992), they present the possibility of producing compassionate understandings that promote effective change and progress (Rorty, 1989).

This is clearly a postmodernism response, making possible the construction of evocative accounts revealing people's concrete, human experience. Performances provide the means of complementing or enhancing reports and presentations by:

- studying the world from the perspective of research participants.
- capturing their lived experience.
- enabling participants to discover truths about themselves and others.
- recognizing multiple interpretations of events and phenomena.
- embedding experience in local cultural contexts.
- recording the deeply felt emotions—love, pride, dignity, honor, hate, envy—and the agonies, tragedies, triumphs, and peaks of human experience embedded in people's actions, activities, and behavior.
- representing people's experience symbolically, visually, or aurally in order to achieve clarity and understanding.

In recent years I have observed some stunning performances that have greatly extended my understanding of people's experience. I have seen class evaluations including poetry, song, role play, and art that provided me with deep insights into the learning experiences of my students, enabling me, as teacher, to extend my thinking about the ways my classes are organized and operate. I have seen the powerful artistic work of small children provide wonderfully illuminative representations of their classroom experience. I have sat in the audience, deeply moved by middle school children's dramatic presentation of an issue touching their school lives. In all these, I have been surprised by the depth and extent of my responses to these performative presentations, feeling deeply "touched" by what I have seen and heard, and more sensitive to the nature of the performers' experiences and how the issues they represent fit within and affect their lives.

Planning Performances: Developing a Script

Performances are built from the outcomes of data analysis, using similar techniques to those used to fashion reports and presentations. Key features and elements provide the material from which a performance is produced, with participants working creatively to develop effective means for representing their experience. These may be constructed as **poems, songs,** or **drama,** or represented as **symbolic** or **visual art.** As with written and other forms of representation, performances need to be conducted with a clear understanding of the *purpose* they wish to achieve with a specific *audience.* Participants should ask: "What do we wish this audience to know or understand? And how might we best achieve that knowledge or understanding through our performance?"

- Identify the **audience** and **purpose**.
- **Identify participants** whose experiences and perspectives are to be represented.
- **Review the data** for each of these participants.
- **Review the categories and issues** emerging from analysis of data for each participant.
- Use categories to **construct a framework** of key features of experiences and perspectives.
- **Write a script,** using units of meaning and/or elements within the data.
- **Review and edit** the script, checking for accurate rendering of participant perspectives and appropriateness to audience.
- **Member check** by having participants read the script.
- **Rehearse** the performance.

Producing Performances

As with any script, there will be decisions to be made about who will perform which roles, how the setting will be designed, what clothing or costumes will be worn, and who will direct the staging of the performance (i.e. take responsibility for overall enactment of the performance).

Rehearsals are an important feature of performances, enabling participants to review the quality and appropriateness of their production and providing opportunities to clarify or modify the script. People will also become familiar with their roles, sometimes memorizing the parts they need to play, though readings may be used effectively where people have minimal time for preparation or rehearsal.

Sometimes action research requires research participants to formulate on-the-spot performances, so that role plays requiring minimal preparation provide an effective means for people to communicate their messages. For this mode of performance, participants should formulate an outline of a script from the material emerging from their analysis, ad-libbing the words as they enact the scene they wish to represent. Role plays are especially powerful when participants act out their own parts, speaking in their own words and revealing, in the process, clear understanding of their own experiences and perspectives.

Video and Electronic Media

Although live performances provide effective ways to communicate the outcomes of research, video and other electronic media offer powerful and flexible tools for reaching more extended audiences. Not only do video productions provide possibilities for more sophisticated performances, but they enable the inclusion of people whose personal makeup inhibits them from participating in live performances. The technology now available enables video productions to be presented on larger screens, to be shown on computer screens, or to be incorporated into more complex online productions.

Dirk Schouten and Rob Watling (1997) provide a useful model for integrating video into education, training, and community development projects. Their process includes:

- making a recording scheme.
- recording the material.
- making an inventory of the material.
- deciding what functions the material will serve in the text.
- making a rough structure for the text.
- making an edit scheme on the basis of the rough structure.
- editing the text.

Although producing a quality video requires high levels of expertise and careful production, current technology enables even amateurs to produce short and effective products. By recording events in schools, research participants can provide engaging and potentially productive productions that extend the potential of their work. This type of recording enables people to provide sometimes dramatic renderings of their experiences, and to engage in forms of research from which they were previously excluded.

Videotaping also provides research participants with a variety of means for storing and presenting their material. Possibilities today include storing productions in videotape form, on CD/DVDs, or within computers, and these can be viewed or transmitted through a variety of media, including video and DVD players, streaming video, and community television. These formats provide the possibility of reaching a wide variety of audiences and using video productions for many effective educational purposes.

Examples of Performances

Case One: Art in the Classroom

An elementary teacher was concerned that the district was cutting funds for art, restricting her possibilities for both teaching art and engaging in art-like activities for student learning processes. She worked with her elementary students, engaging in an extensive exploration of how art was part of their classroom experience. Through extensive dialogue, writing, and drawing, they mapped out the different ways they experienced art and the ways art was incorporated into their learning. By sorting through the information and materials accumulated in this experience, individual students were able to identify important features of their experience of art, and to represent them artistically and in writing. These products were incorporated into a book produced by the class that the teacher intended to have presented to the district superintendent. The class also produced a large mural, to which everyone contributed, using similar materials to represent the class perspective on the issue.

Case Two: Sexual Harassment in School

Following a classroom discussion a teacher met with five of her female middle school students to explore the issue of sexual harassment in their school environment. She facilitated a process of inquiry in which they first spoke of their experiences and perspectives on harassment, then identified key features of that experience. This was extremely helpful in keeping their focus clear and their thoughts manageable. They decided to incorporate boys into their exploration, and extended their understanding of how males are affected by sexually oriented harassment. They wrote a performance piece—"Speaking Out"—based on what they had learned, then made a tryptich—a three-paneled piece—on which the audience could write down their ideas about harassment after the performance. This was performed at the school and later at the university. Three of the students also wrote an article—"Students Against Harassment"—for publication in the monthly school newsletter. By the end of the school year the number of reported incidents of sexual harassment had dropped from four or five each week to one or two every two weeks.

Case Three: A Classroom Opera

Pam Rossi (1997) wrote her doctoral dissertation as a libretto (a script for an opera) based on her work with 31 children in a bilingual grade 1 classroom. The opera, composed by the children and their teachers, describes how the children, in the course of a two-way bilingual program, came to view Spanish, English, and Chinese as among many choices available when creating meaning. By the end of the creation of the opera all the students had achieved some degree of bilingualism. The libretto is comprised of a plot synopsis, a cast of characters, an overture, and a traditional act/scene structure. Pam notes (2000):

The children were participants in a creating, producing, and performing community of inquirers whose interests and ideas informed and contributed to the process and product, making and sharing meaning in a variety of modes. . . . [O]pera is an awakening to multiple literacies through the facilitation of adults who were mutually engaged in a challenging project, shared their expertise and offered the opportunity for guided practice and ongoing critique in different sign systems. [It] is a vehicle for creating synergistic culture with assessment embedded in the process of doing and undergoing, acting and reflecting.

Case Four: Transformative Evaluation

A university professor asked students in his graduate class to reflect on their experience of the class. They interviewed each other in pairs, then identified the key features of their individual experiences collaboratively. Each person used material from his or her own interview to formulate a performance representing the meanings the class had for them. Through poetry, art, song, drama, dialogue, symbolic presentation, and the use of a fractal, each provided a wonderfully descriptive and powerful representation of their experience of learning. The instructor was able to gain deep insights into the types of learning that were important for them, the extent of their feelings of competence, and the features of the class that enhanced their learning. Dialogue following these performances greatly enhanced class members' understanding of their own learning processes, providing ideas they were able to use in their own teaching. It was a dramatic and forceful indication of the way performances might be used to enhance the power and utility of an evaluation process.

Case Five: Quilt-Making: Understanding Teaching History

Ann Claunch (2000), an elementary school teacher, wished to understand how children learned history. Frustrated by textbooks and a curriculum presenting isolated facts along a timeline dissociated from the larger picture of social events, she moved from presenting history inductively, small to large, to a more deductive approach using narratives rather than textbooks in her teaching of history. She used a conceptual plan of a year-long curriculum as a road map to broaden her thinking. Through reflection, dialogue, and review of literature she recorded key features of what she learned as she reformulated her teaching, creating visual representations of her ideas and experience. "Representing my thoughts with images forced me to sort my thinking into concise statements and the artistic representation of understanding paralleled what I had asked elementary students to do in my research." These images were fashioned into a quilt design, providing a unique and informative display of her project.

SUMMARY

Representation: Communicating Research Outcomes

This chapter presents three main formats for presenting the outcomes of research: *written reports*, *presentations*, and *performances*.

These provide evocative accounts enabling empathetic understanding of participant experience. They should:

- clearly and accurately represent participant *experiences* and *perspectives*.
- be constructed to suit specific *audiences* and *purposes*.

Written reports may take the form of *accounts* and *narratives*, *biographies*, or *ethnographies* written as individual, joint, or collective accounts. They may take the form of *informal summary reports* for project participants, *formal reports* for professional and administrative audiences, or *academic reports* for research journals.

Presentations may integrate *a variety of media*, including verbal reports, charts, flow charts, maps, concept maps, art, figures, overheads, audiotapes, and video and electronic presentations.

Performances may include *drama, art, poetry, music,* or other formats. These may be stored, displayed, and presented in a variety of visual, aural, and electronic forms.

Procedures for constructing *written reports*, or *scripts*, for presentations and performances include:

- identifying *audience* and *purpose*.
- selecting participant *perspectives*.
- reviewing the *data*.
- selecting *key features* and *elements* of experience from the analyzed data.
- constructing a *framework/outline* using these features.
- *writing* the report/script.
- *reviewing* and *editing* the report/script.
- *member checking* for accuracy and appropriateness.

REFERENCES

Altheide, D., & Johnson, J. (1998). Criteria for assessing interpretive validity in qualitative research. In N. K. Denzin & Y. S. Lincoln (Eds.), *Collecting and interpreting qualitative materials.* Thousand Oaks, CA: Sage.

Anderson, G., Herr, K., & Nihlen, A. (1994). *Studying your own school: An educator's guide to qualitative research.* Thousand Oaks, CA: Corwin.

Arhar, J., Holly, M. L., & Kasten, W. C. (2000). *Action research for teachers: Traveling the yellow brick road.* Upper Saddle River, NJ: Prentice Hall.

Armstrong, F. (2004). *Action research for inclusive education.* Routledge Falmer. Abingdon, UK.

Astin, A., Banta, T., Cross, P., El-Khawas, E., Ewell, P., Hutchings, P., Marchese, T., McClenney, K., Mentkowski, M., Miller, M., Moran, E. T., & Wright, B. (1996). *Principles of good practice for assessing student learning.* American Association of Higher Education. Washington, DC. Routledge Falmer. Abingdon, UK.

Atkinson, P. (1992). *Understanding ethnographic texts.* Newbury Park, CA: Sage.

Atweh, B., Weeks, P., & Kemmis, S. (2005). *Action research in practice: Partnerships for social justice in education.* New York: Routledge.

Baldwin, S. (1997). High school students' participation in action research: An ongoing learning process. In E. Stringer & colleagues (Eds.), *Community-based ethnography: Breaking traditional boundaries of research, teaching and learning.* Mahwah, NJ: Lawrence Erlbaum.

Barbour, S., & J. Kitzinger (Eds.). (1998). *Developing focus group research: Politics, theory and practice.* Thousand Oaks, CA: Sage.

Bell, J. (1993). *Doing your research project: A guide for first-time researchers in education and social science.* Buckingham: Open University Press.

Berge, B., & Ve, H. (2000). *Action research for gender equity.* Buckingham, UK: Open University Press.

Berger, P., Berger, B., & Kellner, H. (1973). *The homeless mind: Modernization and consciousness.* New York: Random House.

Berger, P., & Luckmann, T. (1967). *The social construction of reality: A treatise in the sociology of knowledge.* Anchor. Garden City, NY.

Block, P. (1990). *The empowered manager: Positive political skills at work.* San Francisco: Jossey Bass.

Bogdan, R., & Biklen, S. (1992). *Qualitative research for education.* Boston: Allyn & Bacon.

Bray, J. L., Lee, J., Smith, L., & Yorks, L. (Eds.). (2000). *Collaborative inquiry in practice: Action, reflection, and making meaning.* Thousand Oaks, CA: Sage.

Brown, A., & Dowling, P. (1998). *Doing research/reading research. A mode of interrogation for education.* London: Falmer.

Brown, T. & Jones, L. (2002). *Action research and postmodernism: Congruence and critique.* Open University Press/McGraw-Hill. Maidenhead, UK.

Burnaford, G. E., Fischer, J., & Hobson, D. (Eds.) (2001). *Teachers doing research: The power of action through inquiry* (2nd ed.). Mahwah, NJ: Lawrence Erlbaum Associates.

Burns, A. (1999). *Collaborative action research for English language teachers.* Cambridge, UK: Cambridge University Press.

Calhoun, E. (1994). *How to use action research in the self-renewing school.* Alexandria, VA: Association for Supervision and Curriculum Development.

Chirban, J. (1996). *Interviewing in depth: The interactive-relational approach.* Thousand Oaks, CA: Sage.

Christiansen, H., Goulet, L., Krentz, C., & Maeers, M. (Eds.). (1997). *Recreating relationships: Collaboration and educational reform.* Albany: SUNY Press.

Christensen, L. (1997). Philosophical and pedagogical development: An ethnographic process. In E. Stringer and colleagues, *Community-based ethnography: Breaking*

REFERENCES

traditional boundaries of research, teaching and learning. Mahwah, NJ: Lawrence Erlbaum.

Claunch, A. (2000). *Understanding teaching history*. Unpublished paper. Albuquerque: University of New Mexico.

Coghlan, D., & Brannick, T. (2004). *Doing action research in your own organization* (2nd ed.). Thousand Oaks, CA: Sage.

Connelly, F., & Clandinin, D.J. (Eds.). (1999). *Shaping a professional identity: Stories of educational practice*. New York: Teachers College Press.

Connery, C. (2003). *Sociocultural semiotic texts of emerging biliterates in non-academic settings*. Ph.D. dissertation. Albuquerque: University of New Mexico.

Cook, T., & Campbell, D. (1979). *Quasi-experimentation: Design and analysis for field settings*. Chicago, IL: Rand McNally.

Creswell, J. (2002). *Educational research: Planning, conducting and evaluating quantitative and qualitative research* (2nd ed.). Upper Saddle River, NJ: Merrill/Prentice Hall.

Darling-Hammond, L., & McLauglin, M. (1995). Policies that support professional development in an era of reform. *Phi Delta Kappan, 76*(8), 597–604.

De Laine, M. (2000). *Fieldwork, participation and practice: Ethics and dilemmas in qualitative research*. Thousand Oaks, CA: Sage.

De Marrais, K. B. (Ed.). (1998). *Inside stories: Qualitative research reflections*. Mahwah, NJ: Lawrence Erlbaum Associates.

Denzin, N. K. (1989a). *Interpretive biography*. Thousand Oaks, CA: Sage.

Denzin, N. K. (1989b). *Interpretive interactionism*. Newbury Park, CA: Sage.

Denzin, N. K. (1997). *Interpretive ethnography*. Thousand Oaks, CA: Sage.

Denzin, N. K., & Lincoln, Y. S. (Eds.). (1998b). *The landscape of qualitative research: Theories and issues*. Thousand Oaks, CA: Sage.

Denzin, N. K., & Lincoln, Y. S. (Eds.). (2005). *Handbook of qualitative research* (3rd ed.). Thousand Oaks, CA: Sage.

Dewey, J. (1916/1966). *Democracy in education*. New York: Macmillan.

Dewey, J. (1930). From absolutism to experimentalism. In G. Adams & W. Montgomery (Eds.), *Contemporary American philosophy* (pp. 13–27). New York: Macmillan.

Edwards, C., Gandini, L., & Forman, G. (1993). *The hundred languages of children: The Reggio Amelia approach—advanced reflections*. Greenwich, CT: Ablex.

Fals-Borda, O., & Rahman, M. (1991). *Action and knowledge: Breaking the monopoly with participatory action research*. New York: Apex.

Feiman-Nemser, S. (2000). *From preparation to practice: Designing a continuum to strengthen and sustain teaching*. Unpublished manuscript. Michigan State University.

Fine, G., & Sandstrom, K. (1988). *Knowing children: Participant observation with minors*. Thousand Oaks, CA: Sage.

Fink, A. (1995). *The survey handbook*. Thousand Oaks, CA: Sage.

Gay, L., Mills, G., & Airasian, P. (2006). *Educational research: Competencies for analysis and applications*. Upper Saddle River, NJ: Merrill/Prentice Hall.

Genat, W. (2006). *Aboriginal health workers: Primary health care at the Margins*. Perth, West Australia: University of Western Australia Press.

Glanz, J. (2003). *Action research: An educational leader's guide to school improvement* (2nd ed.). Christopher Gordon Publishers.

Goodenough, W. (1971). *Culture, language and society*. Reading, MA: Addison-Wesley.

Graue, M., & Walsh, D. (1998). *Studying children in context: Theories, methods, and ethics*. Thousand Oaks, CA: Sage.

Greenbaum, T. (Ed.). (2000). *Moderating focus groups: A practical guide for group facilitation*. Thousand Oaks, CA: Sage.

Greig, A., & Taylor, J. (1998). *Doing research with children*. Thousand Oaks, CA: Sage.

Guba, E., & Lincoln, Y. (1989). *Fourth-generation evaluation*. Newbury Park, CA: Sage.

Haraway, D. (1988). Situated knowledges: The science question in feminism and the privilege of partial perspective. *Feminist Studies, 14*(3), 575–599.

Hawley, W., & Valli, L. (1999). The essentials of effective professional development: A new consensus. In L. Darling-Hammond & G. Sykes (Eds.), *Teaching as the learning profession: A handbook of policy and practice*. San Francisco: Jossey-Bass.

Heath, S. B. (1983). *Ways with words: Language, life and work in communities and classrooms*. Cambridge University Press.

Helm, J. (1999, March). Projects: Exploring children's interests. *Scholastic Early Childhood Today*.

Henderson, J., Hawthorne, R., & Stollenwerk, D. (2000). *Transformative curriculum leadership*. (2nd ed.). Upper Saddle River, NJ: Merrill/Prentice Hall.

Hollingsworth, S. (Ed.). (1997) *International action research: A casebook for educational reform*. London: Falmer.

Holly, M., Arhar, J., & Kasten, W. (2004). *Action research for teachers: Travelling the yellow brick road* (2nd ed.). Upper Saddle River, NJ: Prentice Hall.

Holstein, J., & Gubrium, J. (1995). *The active interview*. Thousand Oaks, CA: Sage.

Horowitz, I. (1970). Sociological snoopers and journalistic moralizers. *Transaction, 7*, 4–8.

REFERENCES

Huffman, J. (1997). *Beyond TQM: Tools and techniques for high performance improvement*. Sunnyvale, CA: Lanchester Press.

Johnson, A. (2002). *What every teacher should know about action research*. Boston, MA: Allyn & Bacon.

Johnson, A. (2007). *A short guide to action research* (3rd ed.). Boston, MA: Allyn & Bacon.

Johnson, B. (2001). Toward a new classification of nonexperimental quantitative research. *Educational Researcher, 30*(2).

Keck, L. (2000). *Children's experience of art in the classroom*. Unpublished paper. Albuquerque: University of New Mexico.

Kelly, A., & Sewell, S. (1988). *With head, heart, and hand*. Brisbane, Australia: Boolarong.

Kemmis, S., & McTaggart, R. (1988). *The action research planner*. Geelong, Australia: Deakin University Press.

Koshy, V. (2005). *Action research for improving practice: A practical guide*. London: Paul Chapman/Sage.

Krueger, R. (1994). *Focus groups: A practical guide for applied research* (2nd ed.). Thousand Oaks, CA: Sage.

Krueger, R. (1997a). *Moderating focus groups*. Thousand Oaks, CA: Sage.

Krueger, R. (1997b). *Developing questions for focus groups*. Thousand Oaks, CA: Sage.

Krueger, R., & Casey, M. A. (2000). *Focus groups: A practical guide for applied research* (3rd ed.). Thousand Oaks, CA: Sage.

Kvale, S. (1996). *Interviews: An introduction to qualitative research interviewing*. Thousand Oaks, CA: Sage.

Lather, P. (1993). Fertile obsession: Validity after poststructuralism. *Sociological Quarterly, 35*.

Lewin, G., & Lewin, K. (1942). Democracy and the school. *Understanding the Child, 10*, 7–11.

Lewin, K. (1938). Experiments on autocratic and democratic principles. *Social Frontier, 4*, 316–319.

Lewin, K. (1946). Action research and minority problems. *Journal of Social Issues, 2*(4), 34–46.

Lewin, K. (1948). *Resolving social conflicts*. New York: Harper.

Lincoln, Y., & Guba, E. (1985). *Naturalistic inquiry*. Beverley Hills, CA: Sage.

Little, J. (1993). Teacher professional development in a climate of educational reform. *Educational Evaluation and Policy Analysis, 15*, 129–151.

Malaguzzi, L. (1995). *The fountains: The unheard voice of children*. Reggio Amelia, Italy: Reggio Children.

Malinowsky, B. (1961). *Argonauts of the West Pacific: An account of native enterprise and adventure in the archipelagoes of Melanesian New Guinea*. New York: E. P. Dutton. (Original work published 1922.)

Marcus, G. (1998). *Ethnography through thick and thin*. Princeton, NJ: Princeton University Press.

Marshall, C., & Rossman, G. (1999). *Designing qualitative research* (3rd ed.). Thousand Oaks, CA: Sage.

McCaleb, S. (1997). *Building communities of learners: A collaboration among teachers, students, families and community*. Mahwah, NJ: Lawrence Erlbaum.

McCracken, G. (1988). *The long interview*. Thousand Oaks, CA: Sage.

McDiarmid, G. (1994). *Realizing new learnings for all students: A framework for professional development of Kentucky teachers*. East Lansing, MI: National Center for Research on Teaching.

McEwan, P. (2000). The potential impact of large-scale voucher programs. *Review of Educational Research, 70*(2).

McLean, J., Herman, J.L., & Herman J.J. (2005). *Improving education through action research: A guide for administrators and teachers* (Roadmaps to success). Thousand Oaks, CA: Corwin Press.

McNiff, J., & Whitehead, J. (2006). *Action research for teachers–A practical guide*. Abingdon, UK: David Fulton Publishers.

McTaggart, R. (Ed.). (1997). *Participatory action research: International contexts and consequences*. Albany: SUNY Press.

Mead, G. (1934). *Mind, self and society*. Chicago: University of Chicago Press.

Meerdink, J. (1999, February). Driving a car for the first time: Teachers, caregivers and a child-driven approach. In *Early Childhood Matters: The Bulletin of the Bernard Van Leer Foundation*, No. 91.

Merriam-Webster Online Dictionary. (2001). Available online at http://www.m-w.com.

Mertler, C. (2005). *Action research: Teachers as researchers in the classroom*. Thousand Oaks, CA: Sage.

Meyers, E., & Rust, F. (2003). *Taking action with teacher research*. Heinemann. Portsmouth, NH.

Milgram, S. (1963). Behavioral study of obedience. *Journal of Abnormal and Social Psychology, 67*, 371–378.

Mills, G. (2007). *Action research: A guide for the teacher researcher* (3rd ed.). Upper Saddle River, NJ: Merrill/Prentice Hall.

Morgan, D. (1997a). *Planning focus groups*. Thousand Oaks, CA: Sage.

Morgan, D. (1997b). *The focus group guidebook*. Thousand Oaks, CA: Sage.

Morgan, D., & Krueger, R. (1997). *The focus group kit: Volumes 1–6*. Thousand Oaks, CA: Sage.

National Board for Professional Teaching Standards. (1994). *What teachers should know and be able to do*. Detroit: Author.

REFERENCES

National Commission on Teaching and America's Future. (1996). *What matters most: Teaching for America's future*. New York: National Commission on Teaching and America's Future.

Noffke, S. (1997). Professional, personal and political dimensions of action research. *Review of Educational Research, 22*. Washington, DC: AERA.

Oleson, V. (1998). Feminisms and models of qualitative research. In N. Denzin & Y. Lincoln (Eds.), *The landscape of qualitative research*. Thousand Oaks, CA: Sage.

Oleson, V. (2005). Early millennial feminist qualitative research. In N. Denzin & Y. Lincoln (Eds.), *Handbook of qualitative research*. Thousand Oaks, CA: Sage.

Oliva, P. (2001). *Developing the curriculum* (5th ed.). New York: Longman.

Oppenheim, A. (1966). *Questionnaire design and attitude measurement*. London: Heinemann.

Pedraza, P., & Rivera, M. (2005). *Latino education: An agenda for community action research*. Lawrence Erlbaum Associates.

Petty, R., (1997). Everything is different now: Surviving ethnographic research. In E. Stringer & colleagues (Eds.), *Community-based research*. Mahwah, NJ: Lawrence Erlbaum.

Pratiss, J. (Ed.). (1985). *Reflections: The anthropological muse*. Washington, DC: American Anthropological Association.

Punch, M. (1994). Politics and ethics in qualitative research. In N. Denzin & Y. Lincoln (Eds.), *Handbook of qualitative research*. Thousand Oaks, CA: Sage.

Reason, P., & Bradbury, H. (2001). *Handbook of action research*. Thousand Oaks, CA: Sage.

Reason, P. & H. Bradbury (2007). *Handbook of Action Research* (2nd ed.). Thousand Oaks, CA: Sage.

Rorty, R. (1989). *Contigiency, irony, and solidarity*. Cambridge, UK: Cambridge University Press.

Rossi, P. (1997, September). Having an experience in five acts: Multiple literacies through young children's opera. *Language Arts, 74*.

Rubin, H., & Rubin, I. (1995). *Qualitative interviewing: The art of hearing data*. Thousand Oaks, CA: Sage.

Sagor, R. (2000). *Guiding school improvement with action research*. ASCD.

Schouten, D., & Watling, R. (1997). *Media action projects: A model for integrating video in project-based education, training and community development*. Nottingham, UK: University of Nottingham Urban Programme Research Group.

Scriven, M. (1981a). *The logic of evaluation*. Inverness, CA: Edgepress.

Scriven, M. (1981b). Summative teacher evaluation. In J. Millan (Ed.), *Handbook of teacher evaluation*. Beverley Hills, CA: Sage.

Selekman, M. (1997). *Solution-focused therapy with children*. New York: Guilford Press.

Silverman, D. (2000). *Doing qualitative research. A practical handbook*. Thousand Oaks, CA: Sage.

Somekh, B. (2005). *Action research (Doing qualitative research in educational settings)*. Open University Press/McGraw-Hill Maidenhead, UK.

Spradley, J. (1979a). *The ethnographic interview*. New York: Holt, Rinehart & Winston.

Spradley, J. (1979b). *Participant observation*. New York: Holt, Rinehart & Winston.

Spradley, J., & McCurdy, D. (1972). Prospect Heights, IL: Waveland Press.

Stake, R. (2005). Qualitative case studies. In N. Denzin & Y. Lincoln (Eds.), *Handbook of qualitative research* (3rd ed.). Thousand Oaks, CA: Sage.

Stein, M., Smith, M., & Silver, E. (1999, Fall). The development of professional developers: Learning to assist teachers in new settings in new ways. *Harvard Educational Review, 69*(3). Fall.

Stringer, E. (2007). This is so democratic: Action research and policy development in East Timor. In P. Reason & H. Bradbury (Eds.), *Handbook of action research*. Thousand Oaks, CA: Sage.

Stringer, E., & colleagues. (1997) (2001). *Community-based research: Breaking traditional boundaries of research, teaching, and learning*. Mahwah, NJ: Lawrence Erlbaum.

Stringer, E., & Genat, W. (1998, January). The *double helix of action research*. Unpublished paper. Qualitative Research in Education Conference, Athens, Georgia.

Sykes, J. (2002). *Action research: A practical guide for transforming your school library*. Libraries Unlimited. Portsmouth, NH.

Tennant, G. (2001). *Six sigma: SPC and TQM in manufacturing and services*. Gower Publishing.

Tomai, D. (2003). *Action research for educators*. Scarecrow Education.

Trinh, T. (1991). *When the moon waxes red: Representation, gender and cultural politics*. New York: Routledge.

Tyler, R. (1949). *Basic principles of curriculum and instruction*. Chicago: University of Chicago Press.

Van Manen, M. (1979). The phenomenology of pedagogic observation. *Canadian Journal of Education, 4*(1), 5–16.

Van Manen, M. (1982). Phenomenological pedagogy. *Curriculum Inquiry, 12*(3), 283–299.

Van Manen, M. (1984). Practising phenomenological writing. *Phenomenology and Pedagogy, 2*(1), 36–39.

REFERENCES

Van Manen, M. (1988). The relation between research and pedagogy. In W. F. Pinar (Ed.), *Contemporary curriculum discourses* (pp. 437–452). Scottsdale, AZ: Gorsuch Scarisbrick.

Van Manen, M. (1990). *Researching lived experience: Human science for an action sensitive pedagogy.* London, Ontario: Althouse Press.

Wadsworth, Y. (1997). *Everyday evaluation on the run* (2nd ed.). St. Leonards, NSW: Allen and Unwin.

Wallace, M. (1998). *Action research for language teachers.* Cambridge, UK: Cambridge University Press.

Weis, L., & Fine, M. (2000). *Speed bumps: A student-friendly guide to qualitative research.* New York: Teachers College Press.

Wiggington, E. (1985). *Sometimes a shining moment: The Foxfire experience.* Garden City, NY: Doubleday.

Wolcott, H. (1994). *Transforming qualitative data: Description, analysis and interpretation.* Thousand Oaks, CA: Sage.

Youngman, M. (1982). Designing and analyzing questionnaires. In J. Bell (Ed.), *Conducting small-scale investigations in educational management.* London: Harper & Row.

Index

Page references followed by "f" indicate illustrated figures or photographs; followed by "t" indicates a table.